D0145070

A CRITICAL EXAMINATION OF STEM

"A much needed critical examination of STEM discourses… This book exposes the myths of scientism and illustrates the importance of metaphors in carrying forward deeply rooted cultural assumptions, informing critical work in education to rethink dominant assumptions in Western industrial culture shaping education in schools, and impacting funding of research and the structures of teacher preparation. Furthermore, it stands to empower educators and teacher educators—and hopefully educational researchers and policy makers—toward recognizing and understanding that the ecological crisis is a cultural crisis."

—John Lupinacci, Assistant Professor, Department of Teaching and Learning, Washington State University, USA

"Dr. Bowers has spent many years promoting critical discussion of cultural blind spots inherent in the STEM disciplines and academia in general. Many of these blind spots are inherent in the way we think and especially in the assumptions we make about the meaning of ideas that have weighted values. Nothing is neutral, and this is one of the first texts that not only emphasizes the problem of scientism and cultural silences, but also gives practical examples and techniques to revealing these blind spots such that constructive discussions of culture and society can begin and develop."

—Richard R. Jurin, Associate Professor, Environmental and Sustainability Studies and Director, Environmental and Sustainability Studies Program, University of Northern Colorado, USA

This critical examination of STEM discourses highlights the imperative to think about educational reforms within the diverse cultural contexts of ongoing environmental and technologically driven changes. Chet Bowers illuminates how the dominant myths of Western science promote false promises of what science can achieve. Examples demonstrate how the various science disciplines and their shared ideology largely fail to address the ways metaphorically layered language influences taken-for-granted patterns of thinking and the role this plays in colonizing other cultures, thus maintaining the myth that scientific inquiry is objective and free of cultural influences. Guidelines and questions are included to engage STEM students in becoming explicitly aware of these issues and the challenges they pose.

Chet Bowers has taught at the University of Oregon and Portland State University, and was granted emeritus status in 1998. He has also written 20 books on the cultural and linguistic roots of the ecological crisis and four books on the cultural transforming nature of the digital revolution.

Sociocultural, Political, and Historical Studies in Education
Joel Spring, Editor

For additional information on titles in the Sociocultural, Political, and Historical Studies in Education series, visit **www.routledge.com/education**.

A CRITICAL EXAMINATION OF STEM

Issues and Challenges

Chet Bowers

Routledge
Taylor & Francis Group

NEW YORK AND LONDON

First published 2016
by Routledge
711 Third Avenue, New York, NY 10017

and by Routledge
2 Park Square, Milton Park, Abingdon, Oxon, OX14 4RN

Routledge is an imprint of the Taylor & Francis Group, an informa business

© 2016 Taylor & Francis

The right of Chet Bowers to be identified as author of this work has been asserted by him in accordance with sections 77 and 78 of the Copyright, Designs and Patents Act 1988.

All rights reserved. No part of this book may be reprinted or reproduced or utilised in any form or by any electronic, mechanical, or other means, now known or hereafter invented, including photocopying and recording, or in any information storage or retrieval system, without permission in writing from the publishers.

Trademark notice: Product or corporate names may be trademarks or registered trademarks, and are used only for identification and explanation without intent to infringe.

Library of Congress Cataloging-in-Publication Data
A catalog record for this book has been requested

ISBN: 978-1-138-65907-0 (hbk)
ISBN: 978-1-138-65908-7 (pbk)
ISBN: 978-1-315-62044-2 (ebk)

Typeset in Bembo
by Apex CoVantage, LLC

Printed and bound in the United States of America by Publishers Graphics, LLC on sustainably sourced paper.

CONTENTS

PREFACE

Reforming science, technology, engineering, and mathematics (hereafter referred to as STEM) in ways that focus on addressing the real-life problems people and businesses face every day sounds both commonsense and in line with the new emphasis on interdisciplinary approaches to learning to conceptualize and solve problems. However, hidden behind this high-sounding rhetoric is the agenda of the powerful elites focused on economic growth, and the further integration of digital technologies into both manufacturing and marketing that will bring more aspects of daily life under the control of the digital revolution. Students will be attracted by the employment opportunities for STEM graduates, which differ radically from the rising levels of unemployment that now reach 40 percent in some countries and age groups. It is projected that by 2018, over 8 million STEM graduates will be needed in the United States, with cloud computing creating over 1.7 million jobs. Great Britain will require 100,000 graduates a year until 2020, and Germany faces a shortage of 210,000 STEM educated workers. Unmentioned is that one of the tasks of STEM graduates will be to introduce efficiencies by computerizing those sectors of the economy that will lead to fewer jobs for those who do not have a technical background.

The shortage of graduates who can bring an integrated understanding of science, technology, engineering, and mathematics to solving problems as we move further into the Digital Age sounds like we are on the cusp of another global emergency—which interestingly enough is framed in a way that totally excludes consideration of the real emergency we face as the carbon dioxide levels are adding to the acidification of the world's oceans, and as climate change triggers fundamental and irreversible changes in the natural systems that an over-populated world now depends upon. The silence on the part of the promoters of the Common Core Curriculum, of which STEM is a part, about how economic growth is to contribute to reducing the human impact on the viability of natural systems is a serious problem. The reformers also lack an interdisciplinary conceptual basis for understanding the interdependent nature of the world's cultural and environmental ecologies. Their continued embrace of the myth of unending economic and technological progress keeps them from even acknowledging the ecological crisis that, in many parts of the world, has turned droughts, extreme weather, and economic dislocations into the new normal. International conflicts as well as the increasing numbers of people migrating across national borders represent the beginning of this new reality.

There is, however, a deeper set of conceptual problems that have been ignored by our educational institutions. For reasons connected to how our taken for granted interpretative frameworks reproduce past misconceptions and silences, which are reinforced by the narrow disciplinary focus required by our universities and other systems of higher education, recognizing the problems will be especially challenging since they were hidden by earlier Western philosophers who turned their misconceptions into the myths that now guide our approach to modernization and development. The dominant myth is that change leads to progress, which has as its corollary that traditions must be overturned. Other supporting myths include the idea of the autonomous individual, that this is a world of things that can be broken into parts, analyzed and re-engineered in ways that improve both efficiency and human control. Other modern myths include that this is a human-centered world, and that the West, with its print-based and now digital systems of cultural storage, represents the latest stage in the process of evolution.

These myths continue to influence the thinking of prominent scientists such as E.O. Wilson, Michio Kaku, Francis Crick, Lee Silver, and Ray Kurzweil who use their reputations as scientists to promote cultural changes that fit their reductionist mix of a progressive and evolutionary paradigm. Their lack of a deep knowledge of the symbolic worlds of different cultures they want to change, including their own culture, is what leads them into the Alice in Wonderland world of scientism. As will be documented in the following chapters, the various expressions of scientism are based on the myth of a linear form of progress. This can be seen in the Promethean role of scientism, as its promoters ignore the most important questions of the day. Not only do their proposals echo the literary genre of science fiction, but their focus on implementing their proposals does not take into account the voices of the people who will be affected by their changes. Equally important is that the myth of progress is so integral to scientism that there is no consideration of what needs to be conserved. But their embrace of the myth of progress is hidden by their continual reference to how their cultural change proposals need to be understood as the outcome of the evolutionary process of natural section. That evolution has led to the diversity of species being ignored by the scientists promoting the Western myth of progress they interpret as justifying imposing upon other cultures the beliefs and values of the West. Instead of promoting cultural/linguistic diversity, they are using Darwin's theory to justify changes that lead to a global monoculture. This fundamental difference is ignored in the messianic approach of the proponents of scientism.

It is important that the STEM curriculum reforms do not reproduce the combination of conceptual limitations and the accompanying hubris that comes from generations of genuine scientific achievements. Socialization to the language that frames thinking, as well as the silences, in the different areas of scientific and technological specializations, is a powerful force that reproduces the old patterns of viewing the local knowledge of communities, and now of the anomic individuals habituated to the lifestyle of endless consumerism, as needing to be scientifically re-engineered.

What is now dawning upon some people who take seriously the reports of environmental scientists who are identifying the parallels between earlier patterns of mass extinctions and today's changes in the global temperatures and in the chemistry of natural systems is that the West's idea of progress is totally misleading. There are others who are rediscovering the importance of the intergenerational knowledge and skills that enable communities to become less dependent upon fossil fuels, and upon an economic system undergoing radical changes that serve the interests of the super-rich, and on the digital technologies that are creating a surveillance culture where people's lives are being turned into data that, in turn, is now monetized. Their turn toward localism that is gaining support in different regions of the world reflects their awareness that the West's approach to technological progress leads to more poverty and dependence upon expert systems that do not take community-centered ecologically sustainable traditions into account.

Technological innovations will continue to be important, and science will be necessary for acquiring a better understanding of local environments and community patterns of mutual support (what can be referred to as the environmental and cultural ecologies), but they need to reflect a paradigm shift in thinking. Instead of being guided by the myth of progress, which leads to viewing traditional/context specific forms of knowledge, skills, and technologies as sources of backwardness, scientists and technologists need to focus on the ecologically sustainable beliefs, values, and patterns of mutual support that are the basis of self-renewing communities. That is, in a world of increasingly degraded natural systems, and given the widespread impoverishment due in part to the transition to a money economy that is accompanied by automation that undermines work opportunities, the challenge today is to engage in a mindful approach to conserving what contributes to an ecologically sustainable future. The view of progress that reflects the Enlightenment philosophers' limited understanding of how their abstract ideas failed to take full account of the conserving role of the DNA in the biological world, and the linguistic/taken for granted patterns of thinking in the world of cultures, now needs to be revised in favor of a way of thinking that balances a concern with conserving as well as promoting changes that further strengthen the viability of natural and cultural systems.

The need to base STEM courses on a conceptual and moral framework that does not take progress for granted, which too often leads to ignoring the wisdom in local knowledge and daily practices, is much easier to write about than to implement in classrooms—especially when most STEM teachers will have been educated by science professors whose careers have been based on the paradigm inherited from the Enlightenment thinkers of the 17th and 18th centuries, and Darwin's theory of natural selection. With the advances in scientific knowledge of the behavior of natural systems, as well as the explosion in cultural changing new technologies, the proliferation of new fields of scientific study has not been matched by keeping scientists current in understanding the symbolic processes of cultural reproduction and change. As I will argue in the following chapters, most scientists are unaware of how their specialized studies have resulted in being caught in a historical lag in understanding cultures as ecologies of language and identity, of the differences in the ecologies of the cultural commons, and of the ideologies that still encode the misconceptions of mainstream Western philosophers. The current widespread silence among scientists on how the technologies of print and now data are undermining the intergenerational oral patterns of cultural renewal is yet another example of their cultural lag.

The market liberal and libertarian inspired forces now promoting the rejection of the scientific consensus that climate change is being accelerated by human activity, especially human activity centered on the global expansion of the industrial/consumer dependent lifestyle, should not be viewed as conserving anything other than their own economic agendas. Unfortunately, few STEM teachers will have acquired from their mentors an understanding of the importance of conserving cultural traditions that are ecologically sustainable; nor are they likely to have learned to recognize the role that language plays in carrying forward (conserving) the misconceptions of the past—which is now a prominent feature of the Orwellian use of political metaphors such as liberal and conservative. One of the contributions of Enlightenment philosophers was the promotion of critical thinking—which, unfortunately, was associated only with promoting progress rather than also being essential to determining which traditions should be intergenerationally renewed.

Just as the Enlightenment philosophers lacked an awareness of how ideas need to be adapted to what is learned from ethnographic studies of local contexts, most scientists—and all the scientists who are promoting various scientism agendas—are unaware of the importance of engaging in what Clifford Geertz (1977) referred to as "thick descriptions" of the otherwise taken for granted cultural patterns that sustain daily life. The questions identified at the end of each section of the chapter titled "Handbook" address what STEM students need to learn about their own cultural traditions that can be made explicit when they are named. Becoming explicitly aware of cultural patterns that previously were taken for granted will in turn provide a basis for assessing what is problematic about various cultural change agendas of scientists whose hubris has led them to ignore the caution that has been a hallmark of scientific inquiry. These discussion questions, which need to be expanded in ways that take account of the diverse cultural backgrounds of the students, will provide opportunities for students to give close attention to the cultural patterns that otherwise are likely to go unnoticed—and to give voice to the issues they see being raised by the proposals of scientists who are promoting some form of scientism. Learning to give critical attention to the cultural patterns that are otherwise not recognized because of their taken for granted status is a much better approach to learning to adopt an anthropological perspective than relying upon textbook accounts of the cultural patterns of other peoples. Like so many print-based accounts, anthropological studies too often appear as abstract and thus unrelated to the real challenge of scientists and technologies—which is to be aware of the taken for granted patterns of one's own culture as well as those of other cultures.

The moral and ecological issues will be more easily recognized when students engage in an ethnography of their own cultural patterns and compare them to the supposedly progressive cultural changes being proposed by scientists. Hopefully, the moral decisions will be framed by a concern with conserving species and habitats, as well as community-centered traditions that reduce dependency upon consumerism. Ethnographies of how the cultural myths of being an autonomous individual in a human-centered world are impacting natural systems need to focus on how the languaging patterns of the culture reproduce the thinking of earlier eras when there was no awareness of environmental limits. The need for such ethnographies may seem unrelated to addressing the cultural/linguistic roots of the ecological crisis, but as STEM students encounter the proposals for bringing the lives of people in line with the view of progress inherent in the thinking of scientism it will be clear that these scientists are ignoring the ecological crisis, as well as the importance of the world's diverse peoples having a voice in determining whether to adopt the cultural changes of outside experts driven by the Western myth of scientific and technologically based progress. Scientism, in a word, parallels the thinking of mainstream Western philosophers whose ethnocentric thinking ignored other cultural knowledge systems as well as how their own thinking is based on an ecology of misconceptions that can be traced back to the ancient mythopoetic narratives that are still part of modern thinking.

It is important to note that my understanding of the many scientists and technologists who lack an understanding of how the cultural ecologies that carry forward the misconceptions of the past, including the idea that the scientific paradigm enables scientists to avoid cultural influences, has not been limited to reading the writings of leading scientists and technologists who have become the leading proponents of scientism. In the course of my international travels over the past 40 years, in which I gave 83 invited talks on the cultural and linguistic roots of the ecological crisis, I encountered both the silences and taken for granted patterns of thinking of the scientists and technologists in the audiences. I have also had extended discussions with scientists who are leading edge thinkers within their specialized fields of research—and who were unaware of the basic reasons for why such a large percentage of the American public is in denial about the cultural influences on an increasingly degraded environment. The scientists' emphasis on objective data, and reliance upon research protocols that supposedly excluded cultural influences, has contributed to the wider misconceptions about the hidden influence of cultural on patterns of thinking. By not challenging the myth that represents languaging processes as functioning as a conduit through which objective data, ideas, research results can be passed to other scientists who are able to hold in check the otherwise hidden cultural influences on their own thought processes, scientists have contributed to the misconceptions held by the larger society.

I was continually aware that students, colleagues, and average citizens found accepting this myth was far easier than acknowledging that the words communicated to others are metaphors whose meaning were framed, in many instances, by the choice of analogs during earlier eras, and that instead of functioning as a conduit for the communication of objective knowledge and the individual's supposedly original ideas, the metaphorical nature of language carries forward the misconceptions of earlier eras when progress rather than an awareness of environmental limits dominated the taken for granted world of the conceptual and economic elites who controlled what constituted high-status knowledge and values. By supporting this myth, as well as ignoring that the printed word and now data make it difficult to recognize that both are part of different linguistic ecologies that have a history, scientists inadvertently crossed over into becoming cultural change agents—which is one of the characteristics of scientism. But how is it possible to explain this at the end of a short talk when scientists have built a career by ignoring the metaphorical nature of language that brings into question the sender/receiver view of language that sustains the myth of objective (cultural free) knowledge? How is it possible to get teachers to take this seriously when they have been indoctrinated into thinking of the printed word as providing objective information and to ignoring that words have a history that reproduce the misconceptions of earlier eras?

What became a special wake-up call about the hubris of scientists whose knowledge of the linguistic colonization of the present by past misconceptions was on par with that of the average person on the street occurred when I was invited to give the opening talk at a conference of scientists from three leading universities in the state. As a result of a series of misjudgments on the part of the people organizing the conference on environmental issues there was total surprise when I focused on such issues as the cultural ecology of language, how print undermines the exercise of ecological intelligence, and the importance of conserving the cultural commons that have a smaller toxic impact. The discussion that followed made it apparent that the level of understanding of such basic cultural issues might have been greater if I had spoken Mandarin. A pattern I have noticed in talking with other scientists, as was confirmed again during the question and answer session after the talk, is that the scientists showed no curiosity about how the metaphorical language, including the dominant root metaphors, reproduce the misconceptions and silences of earlier eras in the culture.

There have been other voices that confirmed my awareness that the scientific paradigm, and now the extension of Darwin's theory of natural selection by several of his more hegemonic followers such as E.O. Wilson and Richard Dawkins, is limited by virtue of the deep cultural assumptions taken for granted within the scientific community. Scientists such as Wes Jackson and science trained Vandana Shiva have called for scientists to recognize the cultural influences on their thinking. Perhaps the most important critique is Wendell Berry's *Life is a Miracle: An Essay Against a Modern Superstition* (2000). While not a scientist himself, but perhaps the most noted cultural/environmental thinker of our day, Berry presents the most thoughtful deconstruction of what he refers to as the epistemological imperialism of Western science. It is hoped that my effort here will not be met by the same silence and intellectual confusion I encountered after my talk at the conferences of environmentally oriented but culturally uninformed scientists and in conversations with other scientists.

1

THE CULTURAL BAGGAGE MOST SCIENTISTS TAKE FOR GRANTED

Not having earned a Ph.D. in one of the sciences may be the reason I am able to recognize the silences and deep taken for granted cultural patterns of thinking that bring into question what many scientists claim on behalf of their mode of inquiry. As the late Carl Sagan put it, "We (scientists) give our highest rewards to those who convincingly disprove established beliefs" (1997, 35). Michael Soulé, the founder and former president of the Society of Conservation Biology, framed the argument somewhat differently by stating that, "Science, as an institution, is self correcting" (1995, 154). A Platonic spell hangs over this statement as though an institution, like one of Plato's eternal forms, has no human origins or active participants. Or perhaps it's another trick of our English nouns that creates the illusion of a mode of inquiry that is entirely uninfluenced by people who function within an ideological framework that has a history and is often misnamed "an institution." I think it is clear that both Sagan, Soulé, and most other scientists hold the view that while some of their colleagues have drifted into the Alice in Wonderland world of scientism, those who stay true to the scientific mode of inquiry are free of cultural influences— and that there are such entities as objective facts, knowledge, and data.

The claim that the scientific method is self correcting suggests the prospect of unending progress. But the reality is more like the Roman god Janus who recognized the possibility that human endeavors can lead at the same time to two radically different futures. The first is that scientists can make their mode of inquiry available to corporations, the military, and the other groups whose primary agenda is making money, expanding the American empire, and perpetuating the cult of constant innovation without asking what is being lost. The other possibility is to use the scientific mode of inquiry to improve human lives, to understand the cultural impacts on natural systems, and to overturn the misconceptions handed down from the past. The constructive uses of science may also lead to understanding how the previous discoveries of science, and the technologies that followed, were based on the misconceptions of earlier eras—a point that led Soulé to suggest indirectly that scientists are engaged in correcting the misconceptions and hubris of earlier scientists.

On the whole, it needs to be remembered that the vast amounts of toxins introduced into the environment, the technologies that have made craft knowledge and skills obsolete (and now even workers), the technologies and market forces that have undermined the diversity of the world's cultural commons, technologies that are moving us into the era of robot warfare, and increasing the efficiency of corporations in exploiting the environment, are all based on knowledge and technologies that were at some point derived from the work of scientists who may have been motivated by different values—even a concern with improving the human condition. Their shared certainty was that they were contributing to social progress.

My task here is not driven by a competing ideological form of hubris, but rather by over 40 years of observing scientists, some having achieved the highest acclaim of their colleagues, who have crossed beyond the boundaries of their field of research and have taken on the role of oracles of future cultural changes based on extrapolations from some field of science. I have also observed how scientists, in becoming complicit in providing the scientific and technical expertise that has furthered the agendas of the industrial system and the defense establishment, unintentionally provided the moral cover for representing their destructive agendas as scientifically based. In spite of this mixed record of achievements the word "science" has acquired a special status among many Americans—a status that has largely eliminated questioning except by ideological and religious fundamentalists. But even these groups understand the importance of obtaining scientific reports that challenge the consensus within the larger body of scientists. For example, scientists such as Wei-Hock Soon of the Harvard-Smithsonian Center for Astrophysics received hundreds of thousands of dollars from corporations and from the Charles G. Koch Charitable Foundation in return for publishing in scientific journals reports that claimed that the release of the sun's energy largely accounts for recent global warming. Earlier, for-hire scientists wrote reports challenging the evidence that connected smoking with cancer. These scientists serve corporate interests by creating doubt in the public's mind about there being a settled consensus within the larger scientific community on causal relationships. This element of doubt, in turn, enables corporations to continue to poison people's lives and to put billions of tons of carbon dioxide into the Earth's atmosphere that is changing the chemistry of the world's oceans.

As I will more fully explain later, with few exceptions the for-hire scientists, who have increasingly adopted the economic values and mode of thinking of the corporate culture, do not possess more than a surface knowledge of their own culture and that of other cultures. Why is this important? This lack of in-depth knowledge, as well as the ways in which the root metaphors of their culture, particularly those that carried forward over hundreds of years the interpretative frameworks and vocabularies that underlie the current myths of progress, individualism, and mechanism they learned during their early years when acquiring the taken for granted patterns of thinking of the larger culture, led to ignoring the importance of the traditions overturned by their innovations. As many scientists have demonstrated, it is easier to adhere strictly to the protocols governing their research than it is to become aware of the deep cultural assumptions they acquired as they tacitly learned to think and communicate in the languaging systems of their culture. Being aware of the traditions they are overturning that are the basis of morally coherent and ecologically sustainable communities has been an even greater challenge for many scientists. Sagan's statement that one of the highest priorities of scientists is overturning established beliefs is another way of referring to the need to replace traditions with what is new, experimental, and more costly.

At one time privacy was regarded as a widely established belief. It was so well established within Western cultures that efforts by governments to disregard this fundamental tradition were viewed as the tactics of a police state. Now the efforts of computer scientists and market forces have led to the loss of personal privacy and now personal security from hackers. Other taken for granted traditions, such as the assumption that it is safe for children to play in open fields, have similarly disappeared as a result of the efforts of scientists to overcome established beliefs and practices—which usually benefits the traditions of corporations ever in search of larger profit margins. For example, the application of Weed B Gon, a herbicide produced by scientists at Dow Chemical that contains the same family of phenoxy chemicals as Agent Orange, now makes many playgrounds unsafe for children to play in. The moral issues surrounding the applied uses of science will be addressed later, but it is important to point out here that the scientists working for chemical companies are too often silent as the industry coalition in which they are employed work behind the scenes to pressure the federal and state legislatures to pass laws that limit restrictions of the uses of their toxic products.

Scientists are not autonomous rational individuals, but rather cultural beings influenced in ways seldom mentioned in university classrooms—including science classes. The continued influence of such taken for granted root metaphors of individualism, progress, and mechanism (with the taken for granted patterns of thinking of many current scientists no longer being guided by the root metaphors of patriarchy and anthropocentrism) led Wendell Berry to observe in *Life is a Miracle: An Essay Against Modern Superstition*, that the record of genuine achievements of modern science may now be outweighed by its destructive and life threatening impacts. In his criticism of E.O. Wilson's claim that the knowledge gained from the sciences "continues to expand globally while passing from one generation to the next," Berry notes that this global expansion of Western knowledge contributes to the loss of local knowledge. A full accounting of the achievements of Western science must also consider the question "what is gained?" when the "immensity of knowledge derived from sciences is measured against its contribution to the immensity of violence" (2000, 90–91).

In addition to acknowledging that my criticisms and suggestions for reform in the education of future scientists are not constrained by the need to win approval from within the scientific community (their judgments cannot affect the reward system of the academy as I am no longer part of that narcissistic culture), I want to make clear what my primary intentions are. They assuredly are not to gain the support of today's wide range of religious fundamentalist and market liberal critics of scientists—particularly of the scientists who are reporting on changes occurring to the world's ecosystems and suggesting that human activity may be the primary cause. These fundamentalist and socially reactionary critics take for granted various religious and ideological Truths, and want to maintain the public policies and personal advantages justified by these Truths.

Given the fundamentalist's friend/enemy way of looking at the world, science as a way of knowing, and not just individual scientists, must be attacked for relying upon a false epistemology—which means that the only knowledge to be taken seriously by these fundamentalists is based on print-based abstractions handed down from the past—and reiterated by the like-minded. For them, knowledge derived from observable evidence is not to be taken seriously. Ironically, the religious and ideological fundamentalists who are now attacking the empirical evidence that represents a consensus among the world's environmental scientists mirror the same cultural patterns established by mainstream Western philosophers and social theorists who helped transform their abstract and culturally uninformed theories into the high status knowledge that is now the basis of a liberal education that traditionally excluded environmental issues.

I hold the opposite view about the Janus nature of abstract knowledge—which means I am also critical of key ideas derived from the writings of such influential philosophers such as Plato, John Locke, Adam Smith, René Descartes, Herbert Spencer, and John Dewey (who was also a Social Darwinian thinker and largely clueless about the nature of traditions). Over time their culturally uninformed theories led to the reification of ideas and values that should not have been understood as universal Truths. Today, these abstract ideas underlie various ideologies held by powerful interest groups and corporations that are the source of employment for the majority of scientists who, partly out of the need to make a living and partly because they share many of the same deep cultural assumptions, promote the environmentally destructive economic and political agenda of corporations and interest groups such as the CATO Institute and Americans for Prosperity. Like so many of the changes in thinking that the ecological crisis challenges us to undertake, we need to move beyond C.P. Snow's 1959 Rede Lecture where he criticized the ignorance that separated the two cultures from each other: that of the sciences and that of the humanities. In light of the deepening ecological crisis, the two cultures now need to be understood as the culture of abstract ideas, information, and data—and the face-to-face, intergenerationally connected cultures that have learned to discriminate between ecologically sustainable and unsustainable changes in the cultural and natural systems upon which they depend. Within this context, it is easier to recognize that the research findings of environmental scientists, as well as warnings about the causal relationships between cultural beliefs and practices and the deepening ecological crisis, must be taken seriously.

At the same time it becomes clearer how much of the legacy of the humanities, particularly the abstract theories of mainstream Western philosophers—including their silences and ethnic prejudices—continue to influence the political and economic agendas that have framed the research of the scientists since the beginning of the Industrial Revolution. As universities now model themselves in accordance with corporate values, and the cultural myths inherited from the philosopher side of the humanities continue to be taken for granted by many scientists, the research agendas of academic scientists are similarly being influenced. Indeed, many of the silences in the writings of mainstream Western philosophers are part of the silences in the education of tomorrow's scientists—which will be addressed later.

One of the purposes of writing this book, rather than spending my last days enjoying the sunsets and reminiscing about past years, is to draw attention to how the scientists' lack of knowledge of their own culture, their complicity in giving scientific legitimacy to the ecologically destructive market system and the equally ecologically destructive military establishment, as well as their increasing tendency to act as oracles of which cultural futures will meet the Darwinian test of natural selection, bring the credibility of scientists into question. These shortcomings serve as evidence for many thoughtful people, as well as for fundamentalist critics, that the research of environmental scientists should not be taken seriously. Ray Kurzweil's (1999) prediction that in the immediate decades ahead super computers will not only replace humans in the process of evolution but will also have religious experiences, and Michio Kaku's prediction that science will give us the power of the gods of mythology . . . "to create life on demand" and to create objects "out of nothing" (2011, 349) can only add to the doubts about the judgments of scientists. Spending billions of dollars on the basic research and technological development to send scientists to Mars and beyond raises further questions about whether their vision of the future is based on an intuitive wisdom the rest of us do not possess, or a special interest in securing future employment as the deepening ecological crisis begins to unravel the market system they so heavily depend upon.

The compromise reached by one mid-West state legislature on whether a discussion of climate change could be allowed in the state approved science curriculum reflects the relativistic thinking that, like a virus, now affects the entire country in thinking about the findings of environmental scientists. The provision in the state approved science curriculum required that students be encouraged to make their *own* decisions about the causes of climate change. In effect, the real message communicated in the science class is that the personal whim and short attention span of students is a more reliable source of knowledge than the consensus of an international body of scientists.

Fundamentalist and market liberal politicians are not the only ones who question the credibility of scientific research. The scientism of E.O. Wilson, Stephen Hawking, and Francis Crick adds to the double bind where their latest personal insights and science-driven agendas for emancipating the public from its own ignorance also raises doubts in the minds of many non-fundamentalists and non-market liberal thinkers. Memories of the scientists' support of the eugenics movement, as well as intelligence testing based on the use of the English language, may have faded, but the latest expressions of scientism again raise the question of whether the guiding ideology of science is inherently self-correcting.

When such acclaimed scientists as E.O. Wilson describe the brain as a machine . . . a problem in engineering (1998, 96, 102); Richard Dawkins explains that "successful genes will . . . postpone the death of their survival machines (human beings are now to be understood as survival machines) at least until after reproduction" (1976, 47–48); Ray Kurzweil claims to have discovered the secret of human thought that will enable him to create a human mind (2012, 281); Stephen Hawking promises that as soon as the "Theory of Everything" can be represented as a mathematical equation humans will understand why they are here (1996, 175); and Francis Crick claims that "when we understand more precisely the *mechanisms* of intuition, creativity, and aesthetic pleasure, and in so doing grasp them more clearly and, it is hoped, enjoy them more" (1994, 261, italics added), it becomes difficult for an outsider such as myself to understand why they have been so highly acclaimed within the scientific community.

The failure to criticize the absurd and dangerous pronouncements of these scientists, which are on par with many of the beliefs held by the religious fundamentalists, is reproduced in the free pass given to the journeyman scientists working on how robots can be used for military purposes, on how to alter the chemistry of the brain so that bad memories can be deleted (which will enable governments to redefine bad memories as those that question governmental policies), on how to narrow the process of learning to what can be tested by computer programs, as well as thousands of other economically and ideologically driven projects that are destructive of communities, natural systems, and the ability to exercise ecological intelligence.

The above predictions by prominent scientists need to be read in light of the title of Carl Sagan's book, *The Demon-Haunted World: Science as a Candle in the Dark* where he writes that, "the reason that science works so well is partly (the) built-in error-correcting machinery. There are no forbidden questions in science, no matters too sensitive or delicate to be probed, no sacred truths" (1997, 34). Sagan's statement not only reaffirms the Promethean mindset of the above scientists, it also reveals a major shortcoming in how many scientists understand the nature of cultural traditions that are to be overturned by scientific advances.

I shall return to the above expressions of hubris when I address what the education of future scientists should include about an aspect of culture about which few scientists are concerned: namely, that what many cultures regard as sacred serves to limit the hubris of humans who assume they have the right to exploit and dominate.

The slowness in the self-correcting nature of science can be seen in the widespread effort to explain all cultural practices as being governed by the forces of natural selection. This tradition began with Herbert Spencer (1820–1905) in the second half of the 19th century when he coined the phrase "survival of the fittest." This conceptual framework continues to be taken for granted today by both libertarian and market liberal thinkers, and it was also used by Nazi scientists as the moral basis for exterminating millions of people they regarded as less fit. Spencer's catchy phrase has now been replaced by referring to the "better adapted"—which still can be interpreted as encoding the moral guidelines for how the less well adapted should be treated. The conceptual foundations of Darwin's theory have been further expanded in ways that make the process of natural selection more inclusive—not only of values but also the arts and aesthetic experiences generally (Dissanayake, 1990, 1995). E. O. Wilson and Richard Dawkins have popularized the new metaphor of "meme," which they claim plays the same evolutionary role in cultures that genes play in the biological world. The computer scientists now reducing the world's knowledge and rich heritage of intergenerational knowledge to what can be reduced to context-free and supposedly objective information and data are also invoking Darwin's theory to justify their efforts to eliminate the less fit ways of knowing—which happen to be oral tradition-centered cultures (Stock, 1993; Moravec, 1990; Kurzweil, 1999, 2005, 2012; Dyson, 1998). The question that now needs to be asked is: Where are the critical voices of scientists who function as the self-correcting *machinery* of science as an institution—to mix the metaphors of Sagan and Soulé?

The above examples of how scientists occupying the top rungs of the science pyramid, in continually going beyond their areas of expertise by entering the realm of scientism that discredits the legitimate gains of scientific knowledge, points to the basic limitations of past and current approaches to the education of scientists and technologists. Before suggesting how to correct these limitations in the education of the next generation of scientists, it is first necessary to provide a way of understanding how I view the importance of taking seriously the findings of environmental research, especially the changes in the chemistry of the world's ocean, including the changes in habitats as well as in the potential release of green house gases such as methane that could raise global temperature between 4 and 5 degrees Celsius.

The danger today is that the efforts to make science the "candle in the dark," as Sagan put it, and to base the "consilience" of all cultural ways of knowing and valuing on what can be scientifically tested and proven, as advocated by E. O. Wilson, is that they introduce the friend/enemy distinction into the public discourse when, in reality, the most basic issues today are related to how to live in ways that are less environmentally destructive. Prominent scientists such as E. O. Wilson, Francis Crick, and Richard Dawkins are leading the charge, that includes lesser known scientists, to replace what they claim are the less well adapted world religions with what their critics view as the religion of science— which now claims we are entering the post-biological phase of the evolutionary process. In place of religions (not all of which have the idea of a patriarchal God in the sky who oversees all life and determines who merits a free pass into heaven), E. O. Wilson claims that scientists are best qualified to determine the values that humanity should live by. He explains their Promethean role, "science for its part will test relentlessly every assumption about the human condition and in time uncover the bedrock of moral and religious sentiments" (1998, 265).

Lee Silver, a professor of molecular biology and public policy at Princeton University and a Fellow of the American Association for the Advancement of Science, goes further in his book, *Remaking Eden: How Genetic Engineering and Cloning will Transform the American Family* (2007), by explaining how technology now enables humans to take control over their own evolution. Genetic engineering now holds the possibility of creating a GenRich segment of the population that will control all aspects of the economy, the media, and the entertainment and knowledge industries.

The Naturals who will make up 90 percent of the population will continue to provide the hard labor that will provide the basic services and sources of protein. Silver did not anticipate that his colleagues working on robot intelligence were already envisioning the elimination of the Naturals that are to make up the larger segment of Silver's utopian world. But he was correct in anticipating that the scientists' drive to achieve control over human destiny by using genome-editing techniques would not disappear. Powerful market forces and the desire to enhance the genetic potential of one's offspring would further support what the elite within the scientific community already assumed to be the direction that future progress will take. There may be, from time to time, calls for a moratorium on the use of genome editing technologies, but there are so many cultural variables that are outside the control of scientists that, as Jacque Ellul notes in *The Technological Society* (1964), there is little evidence in the West that new technologies are permanently rejected. Scientists, including those conducting experiments on prisoners in Nazi concentration camps such as Ravensbrück, demonstrated how an ideologically driven zeal for new knowledge can lead to immoral ends that go unquestioned by other scientists who share the same cultural assumptions. Just as Wilson, Crick, the computer scientists, and futurist-thinking theoretical physicists such as Kaku envision the new scientific breakthroughs as leading only to progress; they all share an inability to consider, in light of the ecological crisis, the cultural traditions that need to be intergenerationally renewed (that is, conserved).

We are now learning that much of what we encounter in today's media is written by what is being called "automated narrative generation." That is, algorithms and natural language generators now produce written content that has all the appearance of being authored by humans. Given the authority that the printed word has for many people who are too busy to check out whether the narrative was written by a human or by a robot, and given the vast number of robo-written newspaper accounts, and even books, what assurances do any of us have that the instructions guiding the new gene editing technologies, the use of military robots, and decisions about what constitutes a correct test score have not been produced by computer algorithms? The scientists' unending quest for perfection, ever greater efficiency and profits, have now largely made humans, democracy, and the genuine achievements of the past increasingly irrelevant.

A more balanced way of understanding both science and technology, especially the digital technologies that are changing the world in fundamental and irreversible ways, is to think of them as having the characteristics of the ancient Roman god, Janus. In Roman mythology, Janus was the god of doorways and the patron of all new undertakings. Janus was visually represented as having two faces looking in opposite directions. Thinking of the Janus nature of science and technology puts the focus on how science is always entering new doorways to knowledge, and the potential of new cultural beginnings. That the two faces look in opposite directions highlights the possibility of new beginnings leading to destruction as well as to the renewal and transformation of life. Unlike the current Western myth that associates change with a linear form of progress, thinking of the Janus nature of science and technology leads to asking questions that require a deep knowledge of culture's traditions and whether these traditions strengthen or diminish the prospects of a sustainable future.

If we consider the recent history of science and technology we can see they have had an uneven record, with it now being difficult to determine, for example, whether the destructiveness of the toxic impact on the health of natural systems now exceeds their contribution to the quality and sustainability of living systems. Unfortunately, the Janus nature of the highly publicized gains and largely unrecognized losses associated with the globalization of the digital revolution may have moved beyond the point where the loss of the largely non-monetized intergenerational knowledge and skills essential to the well-being of the world's diversity of cultural commons will make it impossible to reverse course.

2

AVOIDING THE SEPARATION OF SCIENCE AND CULTURE

The globalization of the industrial/consumer dependent culture that is changing the chemistry of the world's natural systems, as well as a world population that has expanded by nearly 6 billion people over the last century, points to a basic reality that needs to be taken into account in the education of the next and possibly last generation of scientists and technologists. That is, the margin for errors is being radically reduced as meeting the basic needs of 7 billion people is already destroying the natural systems necessary for sustaining life. In addition to oceans becoming more acidic and being over-fished, forests are disappearing that previously served as important habitats and as carbon sinks, and now the world faces the prospect that the high rate of warming of the Arctic may release vast amounts of methane gas that will send the world's temperature soaring. One of the most important implications for thinking about the education of the next generation of scientists is that they must learn to differentiate between the uses of scientific knowledge that promote ecologically sustainable cultural ways of thinking and practices, and those that are driven by the deep and largely taken for granted cultural assumptions inherited from the past that did not (and still do not) take account of environmental limits.

What most upper grade school and high school students will learn from their first science class is the 17th-century way of understanding the scientific mode of inquiry. It will be explained as putting in check previous cultural misunderstandings and then engaging in careful observation, measurement (including the collection of data and written descriptions), conducting experiments to test and then formulating and even modifying a hypothesis (explanatory framework). The method will also be explained to students as relying upon observable and measurable evidence that is open to revision. Unfortunately, there is unlikely to be an in-depth discussion of the nature of traditions and the many ways they are carried forward—even in the thinking of scientists.

This first introduction to learning the scientific mode of inquiry will also involve adopting another carry over from the early 17th-century scientists such as Johannes Kepler. That is, the emphasis on examining phenomena, from that of a frog to that of how chemical changes affect organic processes, will involve a mechanistic pattern of thinking where the phenomena are broken into their many parts, with the focus then shifting to how they interact with each other. This mechanistic interpretative framework promotes experimentation where changes in the parts can be observed and the outcomes can be measured—with the entire process being governed by the values of achieving greater efficiency and prediction. It is unlikely that the steps to the scientific method will receive more than a quick overview, as the emphasis will be on engaging students in observations of actual life forming and sustaining processes, giving close attention to gathering data or careful descriptive accounts, and, at a higher level, forming a hypothesis and then checking it in terms of observable evidence.

What few science teachers will explain to students is that these steps, the mechanistic interpretive framework, and the emphasis on observable and measurable evidence, are based on Western assumptions and that these assumptions differ from the assumptions of other cultures that developed approaches to observing, interpreting, and predicting the behavior of life processes based on their own mythopoetic narratives. This failure to mention that what is now termed modern science is a culturally specific way of knowing, and while it has been highly successful in understanding and predicting how the natural forces can be used to achieve predictable outcomes, it will also be accompanied by another silence that still goes unexamined by scientists whose achievements have been widely acclaimed.

That is, this silence has to do with the implications of elevating the West's scientific knowledge over the knowledge of other cultures—many of which acquired a deep knowledge of the natural systems they have carefully observed for many generations. This 17th-century hold-over of promoting a mechanistic interpretative framework that excluded what cannot be empirically observed and subjected to experimentation and measurement (and which was based on the misconception of autonomous entities) also leaves students with a basic misconception that will likely stay with them throughout their careers as scientists—as can be seen in the thinking of most current scientists. That is, students will learn that their mode of inquiry is free of cultural influences—including cultural values and both ancient and modern mythopoetic narratives. This leads to young and later well established scientists assuming that their experiments are free of cultural influences, even though their experiments and technologies too often have an unrecognized cultural transforming impact.

As the scientific mode of inquiry is often understood as being unable to address questions of values, some scientists have held that they are not responsible for the moral issues that arise when their discoveries and the resulting technologies are misused or lead to unanticipated consequences such as we are now experiencing with how complex digital systems can be taken over by hackers. It is hard to believe that scientists working for Dow Chemical, Monsanto, and the hundreds of other corporations that have saturated the environment with toxic chemicals are not aware of the human deformities and serious health issues to which their research contributes. Their primary defense is to claim that their moral responsibility does not extend to how others use their discoveries.

There are also unrecognized moral issues when Western scientific/technological advances are promoted in other cultures as the latest expression of modern development and progress. Instead of understanding the Janus nature of the chemical pesticides and fertilizers that made possible the Green Revolution in India and elsewhere in the so-called under-developed world, which would have led to considering the degradation of soils, pollution of local ecosystems, and the extra financial burden that is now leading to a high level of suicides today among Indian farmers, only the higher yields were recognized. The discovery of DDT's potential as an insecticide by Paul H. Müller (for which he earned a Nobel Prize in 1939) was for many years understood as yet another example of the progressive nature of science. Scientists initially resisted taking seriously what Rachel Carson documented in *Silent Spring* (1962) about its destructive impact on the reproductive capacity of birds. Similarly, the digital technologies that now create the near total surveillance networks that benefit corporations and governments, and undermine the intergenerational traditions of knowledge passed forward through face-to-face communication and through the vernacular languages, are being promoted by scientists who lack an understanding of the cultures into which their technologies are being introduced. This lack of awareness of the cultural traditions being overturned by the digital revolution leaves them unable to recognize whether they are contributing to or undermining ecologically sustainable lifestyles.

The indifference to recognizing the cultural roots of the scientific method, and the indifference to other cultural ways of knowing displaced by the hegemony of Western science and technology, as well as the myth that scientists are free of cultural influences, now needs to be addressed by radically enlarging the scope of science education. Without understanding the many ways in which both the Western approaches to science and technology are driven by specific cultural assumptions and market forces, as well as how these underlying assumptions are undermining the conceptual and moral foundations of their own culture as well as that of other cultures, the Janus nature of science and technologies will continue to shift more in the direction of being a destructive force. As the sociologist Edward Shils (1981) points out, Western science and technology share many assumptions of the Enlightenment thinkers who equated progress with overturning traditions—regardless of the merits of the traditions. Science, as Shils notes, is an anti-tradition tradition that is clearly embraced by Sagan when he claims that "we give our highest rewards to those who convincingly disprove established beliefs" (1997, 35).

3

AN OVERVIEW OF WHAT SCIENTISTS NEED TO KNOW ABOUT THE CULTURES THEY ARE TRANSFORMING

The word "overview" is the key word here, as the overview is intended to provide a broad conceptual framework that will enable the classroom science teacher to recognize how the different dimensions of cultures, for which there will be in-depth descriptions in following chapters, can be introduced in students' STEM classes. Introducing students to the scientific mode of thinking, at least in the early stages, seldom makes a distinction between science and the uses of technologies as most classroom teachers share the popular misconceptions about technology being a culturally neutral tool to be used to achieve the outcomes desired by its users. There will be more later on the implications of this misconception, which can be found in the thinking of most scientists—and in particular the computer scientists. (Are they really scientists or primarily technologists who rely upon mathematics, physics, and the scientific gaze to perfect their technologies?)

Students' initial encounter with learning from experiences that carry the label of science education should begin with an explanation that every aspect of scientific inquiry is influenced by cultural assumptions and patterns of interaction. This will require a brief explanation of cultural and patterns of interaction, which can best be done by having students consider cultural patterns they reenact on a taken for granted basis. This, in turn, will require an explanation of what is meant by "taken for granted." Taken for granted aspects of culture can be named in ways that students will recognize if examples of gender bias are introduced, if the assumptions about the differences between what is spoken and what is encoded in print (and which has the greater authority?) are discussed by students. Often-used phrases such as "our world," "mankind," "I think," and "objective knowl-edge," can be discussed in terms of the hidden cultural assumptions, the historical and culturally specific origins (which the teacher will need to be able to intro-duce), and the really big question that can be introduced later in the students' education: Can we think and communicate without relying upon the vocabulary inherited from earlier generations who were unaware that the vocabularies they took for granted had an even earlier and culturally specific history?

What other aspects of the science/technology curriculum are influenced by taken for granted cultural assumptions and patterns of interaction? This question can be explored in a number of ways that make explicit how scientists, ranging from pure to applied science, are dependent upon cultural/linguistic patterns ignored by their mode of inquiry. For example, what are the cultural traditions scientists rely upon when they explain the nature and importance of their research, as well as the nature of the evidence and data that support the outcome of their research? Do they rely upon traditional spellings of words, the conventions of writings that replicate oral patterns where pauses and shifts in tone of voice make certain thoughts and insights stand out from the rest? That is, do scientists rely upon the use of paragraphs, capitalizations, use of third person reporting, standard spellings that reproduce the shortcomings in the Western ecology of spelling? Do they organize their ideas in terms of the subject, verb, object pattern of thinking, writing, and communicating? Do they take for granted the 17th-century Enlightenment assumptions that built on the earlier assumptions about the rational process being free of cultural influences—an assumption that easily leads, as both John Locke and René Descartes put it, to the idea that "individual thinking" (which itself is based on a cultural misconception) should be understood as free of historical influences. The ideas of "objective knowledge," and now "data," also have a history that can be traced back to earlier Western elite thinkers who were successful in getting succeeding generations to accept their choice of analogs that continue to frame the current meaning of these words. Is the scientist who takes for granted what these two metaphors exclude, which includes the whole range of cultural influences, being influenced by cultural traditions that the scientific mode of inquiry fails to acknowledge? Other traditions that scientists were slow to recognize include how their early medical research used the male as the model for the testing of new drugs, and until even more recently there was the long held bias against female scientists that discouraged young women from pursuing science as a career.

That scientists cannot escape cultural influences on their ways of thinking, and their approaches to the development and uses of technologies, must also take account of how their taken for granted ways of thinking about the languaging processes of their own cultures influence their prejudices toward other knowledge and values systems. When reliance upon the scientific mode of inquiry first emerged in the West, it was viewed as providing the knowledge and technologies necessary for beating the wildness out of nature and turning it into an exploitable resource. In recent years, with the introduction of the vocabulary that supported thinking of nature as diverse, interacting and interdependent ecologies, the focus of research and the development of technologies underwent profound changes—except for the branches of science and technology that provided the innovations required by the industrial and now digital revolutions.

During my 40-some years of thinking and writing about the cultural/linguistic roots of the ecological crisis, I have read many of the most highly acclaimed scientists from a variety of fields, and I have had surprisingly strange conversations with scientists that reflected a critical silence in the educational process they underwent as graduate students. This silence is one that is also shared by people who have been mis-educated about one of the most important characteristics of their culture. That is, there is a wide range of cultural practices that reinforce the idea of thinking of language as functioning as a conduit through which ideas, information, and now data can be sent to others. This conduit (sender/receiver) view of language as well as the process of encoding in print what are actually linguistically influenced interpretations reinforce the ideas of objectivity, factualness, and universalism—while hiding the ecology of human/cultural authorship, the ecologies of cultural contexts, and other cultural ways of knowing.

The conduit view of language is absolutely essential to maintaining the myth of objective knowledge that is derived from supposedly culturally unmediated empirical investigations—as though there is no cultural being called a "scientist" who is observing, measuring, predicting, excluding, and putting it all down in print or in other visual systems of representation that will lead to building up the record of publications in refereed journals necessary for academic promotion. When research appears in print, which reinforces the conduit view of language, and the author sustains the myth of objective knowledge by writing in the third person that avoids any references to the personal feelings, memories, intuitions, and, sense of achievement that is part of the research project, there is another taken for granted cultural pattern that most scientists are unaware of reinforcing. One of the characteristics of the printed word, especially when used in the cultural context of scientific research or of "objective" reporting as found in the various media, is that the histories of words are ignored. Words such as "data," "progress," "individualism," "behavior," "evolution," "intelligence," and so forth are assumed to refer to real entities, events, relationships, and ideas. The mis-education of most scientists, as well as the general public, has led to ignoring that nearly their entire vocabulary, excluding prepositions and conjunctions, are metaphors, and that many of current meanings of words that supposedly convey an individual's thoughts and insights were framed by analogs settled upon in the distant past. The reduction of cultural contexts, embodied experiences, and the exercise of culturally mediated intelligence to the objective status of "data" or the printed word appearing on a page or screen further hides the taken for granted cultural traditions.

Not only are words such as "woman," "data," "progress," "research," "technology," "wilderness," and "environment" metaphors, but their meanings continue to be framed in the West by root metaphors derived from the culture's mythopoetic narratives, powerful evocative experiences, and the steady stream of examples that appear on the surface to support the explanatory framework of root metaphors such as progress and mechanism. The most prominent root metaphors (that is, conceptual frameworks) that scientists took for granted for hundreds of years included patriarchy and anthropocentrism—with both now being questioned. The other prominent cultural shaping root metaphors still taken for granted by scientists include mechanism, individualism, progress, evolution, and now ecology. The latter root metaphor is now leading environmental scientists to question the patterns of thinking and values based on the root metaphors of mechanism, individualism, progress, and economism. These root metaphors provided the conceptual and moral legitimacy for the Industrial Revolution that is now in its digital stage of development.

As a taken for granted interpretative framework, the 17th-century root metaphor of mechanism continues to frame the thinking of scientists in a variety of fields, ranging from genetic research, understanding the complexity and processes of the brain, to computer science. What is important to recognize is how the vocabulary of mechanism provides the basic conceptual and moral framework in a variety of cultural areas—which now extends into the fields of medicine, agriculture, education, business, and the digital revolution with its coming Internet of Everything. The connections being made between a mechanistic interpretive framework and the idea of scientific progress were widespread in the early 17th century, with Francis Bacon's *New Atlantis* representing the utopian future where science would provide complete control over nature and the organization of society. Here I shall use a statement by Johannes Kepler that best summarizes the root metaphor of a mechanistic universe, followed by how other leading thinkers of their times relied upon it to explain other aspects of life ranging from the political, creative, educational, to evolution itself.

Analogies that Encode the Root Metaphor of a Mechanistic World

> My aim is to show that the celestial machine is to be likened not to a divine organism but to a clockwork.
>
> (Johannes Kepler, 1571–1630)

> For what is the heart, but a spring; and the nerves, but so many strings; and the joints, but so many wheels, giving motion to the whole body . . .
>
> (Thomas Hobbes, from the *Leviathan,* 1651)

> Our conscious thoughts use signal-signs to steer the engines in our minds, controlling countless processes of which we're never much aware.
>
> (Marvin Minsky, from *The Society of Mind,* 1985)

Like the computer, the human mind takes in information, performs operations on it to change its form and content, stores information, retrieves it
when needed, and generates responses to it.

(Anita Woolfolk, from *Educational Psychology*, 1993)

The would-be writer in need of an idea can hop on the elevator and ride to
the third floor where the 'splot' machine is waiting to offer a creative spark.
Each pull of the handle delivers a randomly generated wacky sentence,
some even illustrated, to provide that creative starting point for the story.

(*Creative Writer*, 1994, software program produced by Microsoft)

But another general quality that successful genes will have is a tendency to postpone the death of their survival machines at least until after
reproduction.

And later in the chapter on "The Survival Machine":

Survival machines began as passive receptacles for the genes, providing
little more than walls to protect them from the chemical warfare of their
rivals and the ravages of accidental molecular bombardment.

(Richard Dawkins, *The Selfish Gene*, 1976)

The machine the biologists have opened up is a creation of riveting beauty.
At its heart are the nucleic acid codes, which in a typical vertebrate animal
may comprise 50,000 to 100,000 genes.

(E. O. Wilson, *Consilience*, 1998)

This root metaphor not only frames how to think about a wide range of cultural
and biological life forming and sustaining processes, but it also excludes other
vocabularies that would lead to very different understandings. The interpretative
frameworks of non-Western culture are excluded, as well as other ways of thinking that have not entirely disappeared in the West.

The continued reliance upon this root metaphor can be seen in the following
explanation of how the brain works.

Neuronal cell bodies . . . are the electrochemical, digital on-off switches
connected by their axonal 'wires' in an intricate network inside your head.
There are billions of neurons in the human brain and each one can connect
with tens of thousands of others, making *trillions* of connections. By inter-
connecting, groups of neurons create neural networks that produce every
conscious and unconscious impulse, response, or thought you may have . . .

(Nichols, 2014, 35)

The question not being asked by scientists working within this conceptual frame-work, including the neuroscientists dependent upon MRI machines that provide the supposedly visual evidence of how the areas of the brain light up during different states of consciousness is: where did scientists acquire the mechanistic conceptual framework, its supporting vocabulary, as well as the either/or pattern of thinking that allows them to exclude cultural influences? Did they learn this mechanistic conceptual framework as part of their professional studies? Does the over-reliance upon machines lead to representing the brain as like a machine—or did the mechanistic root metaphor marginalize awareness of cultural/linguistic influences? The irony is that the mechanistic root metaphor excludes a common sense understanding of the linguistic ecology within which we live: namely, how we acquire a metaphorical vocabulary and the accompanying interpretive frame-works as we become members of our home language community. The linguistic cultural ecology influences the taken for granted conceptual patterns of the cul-ture, including the misconception that words refer to real things—rather than as cultural influenced constructs that too often become reified.

This view of language, it needs to be noted, is essential to maintaining the explanatory power of other root metaphors such as individualism and progress. It is also essential to maintaining the modern myth of objective knowledge and a rational process that is free of cultural influences. One more example of how the vocabulary that supports a mechanistic interpretation of life forming process eas-ily leads to an engineering agenda where efficiency, control, and profits become a major concern can be seen in the vocabulary used to introduce students to the basic "components" of a plant cell. As environmental science students reported back to me while taking my class on the metaphorical nature of thinking, a text-book used in the course they were assisting identified the plant cell as having a "recycling center," a "solar station," a "powerhouse," "production centers" and "storage sacs." The instructor in the course did not raise questions about what is problematic about using a machine-derived vocabulary to describe an organic process.

The mechanistic root metaphor leads to an engineering approach where mea-surement, experimentation, progress in increasing efficiency and yields, and prof-its become primary concerns. It also represents an anthropocentric world, which has been another dominant root metaphor in the West, where humans (including scientists) stand outside rather than being part of the emergent, relational, and co-dependent cultural and natural ecologies. By adopting the Cartesian gaze of an external world they are able to ignore how their own identities, ways of think-ing, values, and silences are influenced by the information circulating through the information pathways that sustain the cultural and natural ecologies that are part of their embodied experiences.

Scientists have been inventive in popularizing new image metaphors that pro-vide a surface knowledge of phenomena they only partially understand, such as "dark matter," "black holes," "big bang," "theory of everything", and so forth.

But the education of most Western scientists, as I have found from attempting to talk with scientists well advanced in their careers about how the metaphorical nature language that encodes the analogs settled upon in earlier eras, continues to be part of their taken for granted linguistic inheritance they fall back on when describing cultural changes. The writings of scientists who have crossed over into scientism continue to ignore the powerful cultural/linguistic influences that cannot be eliminated no matter how rigidly they hold to the ideology that represents their mode of inquiry as free of cultural influences.

There are other deep psychological as well as professional forces that keep scientists from drifting off the mutually reinforcing conceptual/grant generating reservations when it should be obvious that language has a cultural history, that traditions need to be recognized and evaluated in terms of contributing to ecologically sustainable lifestyles as natural systems head toward collapse, and that culturally/ideologically influenced interpretations of Darwin's theory of natural selection and now the increased reliance upon Big Data will not lead to the values that strengthen communities of mutual support and self reliance. Perhaps the most persistent and unrecognized force sustaining ecologically problematic beliefs held by many of today's scientists is what Friedrich Nietzsche referred to as the will to power expressed in "the need to interpret, to name and categorize, and to take control, that drives the quest for knowledge of how the world works" (Kaufmann, 1968, 266–281). The indifference I have encountered among scientists about how the root metaphors, as well as the analogs inherited from the past, continue to frame the meaning of much of today's vocabulary, reproduce the misconceptions and silences of earlier eras when there was no awareness of environmental limits must also be understood as the expression of a will to power to sustain the scientists' role in sustaining the anti-tradition tradition paradigm inherited from the Enlightenment. That is, the will to power is the motivating force in avoiding the uncertainties of a paradigm shift that would result from relying upon the root metaphor of ecology for understanding the cultural transforming and conserving processes that must now be undertaken.

4

THE CULTURAL MEDIATING NATURE OF TECHNIQUE AND TECHNOLOGIES

Another Area of Silence in the Education of Western Scientists

Early in my study of how cultural values and beliefs, and the deep assumptions upon which they are based, influence the self-identity and taken for granted patterns of thinking of the so-called autonomous individual, I learned that some of the most formative assumptions of the culture are introduced in highly simplistic ways in the early grades, and not revisited until graduate school—which too often does not occur. Technologies such as the use of the printed word and the techniques for decoding it, as well as how to think about progress, success, competition, intelligence, individualism, the autonomous nature of things, ideas, and so forth are all introduced in the early grades. Children's books, so heavily loaded with nouns that misrepresent what is actually an emergent and relational world, are a powerful source of indoctrination that even the most highly educated are unable to recognize—which means they carry forward the myth that there are autonomous ideas, individuals, values, data, and so forth. Learning to think of technology as a tool that people use to achieve certain outcomes is also learned in the early grades. The analogs are generally derived from the student's immediate experiences, which means the concepts are vastly oversimplified and represent the ethnocentrism of the dominant culture's representative—the classroom teacher.

The writings of prominent scientists such as Francis Crick, E.O. Wilson, Carl Sagan, Stephen Hawking, Michio Kaku, Howard Fields, Ray Kurzweil, are typical of most scientists whose thinking reproduces many of these and other simplistic explanations acquired in the earliest stages of formal education. These taken for granted patterns of thinking may remain unquestioned over the lifetime of the scientists for the following reasons: their vulnerability during their early stages of language acquisition that provided the initial interpretative frameworks, the lack of alternative vocabularies that would provide the basis for questioning the analogs that become the initial basis for thinking, simplistic questions asked by teachers and significant others which further cement the authority of surface knowledge, the many ways the cultural assumptions and analogs are continually reinforced through interactions with the taken for granted world of significant others, and the ways in which the early stages of developing an interpretative framework provide a seemingly solid and non-problematic conceptual basis for focusing on the more challenging issues that arise as one goes deeper into one of the sciences.

Earlier, I suggested that the scientific method does not take account of how most scientists continue to reproduce what they learned in the earliest grades that represent traditions as sources of backwardness and how critical thinking can lead to original ideas that can then be encoded in words and communicated to others who will understand them as objective facts and information rather than as culturally and too often ideologically influenced interpretations. The mythic nature of the objective gaze of the scientists, even her/his use of both social techniques that are the basis of research protocols, and the mechanical technologies that supposedly limit the intrusion of cultural influences on the outcome of the research, begin to further unravel when we consider the silences and misconceptions about the nature of techniques and technologies that are so prominent among scientists. This may appear as a too sweeping and thus unwarranted generalization, but my criticism can be easily verified by checking how many scientists have read Jacques Ellul's *The Technological Society* (1964); Lewis Mumford's *Technics and Civilization* (1934), *Technics and Human Development* (1967) and *The Pentagon of Power* (1970); Martin Heidegger's *The Question Concerning Technology and Other Essays* (1977); Don Ihde's *Technics and Praxis* (which is his interpretation of Heidegger's classic) (1979); Walter Ong's *Orality and Literacy: The Technologizing of the Word* (1982); Eric Havelock's, *The Muse Learns to Write* (1986).

A strong case can be made that the cultural mediating characteristics of different technologies, which vary from culture to culture, are not adequately understood by scientists. And if this is not understood, the fall back level of understanding is not too far removed from how young students are told by naive classroom teachers that both techniques and technology are in themselves culturally neutral tools and at the same time the engines of progress. Modern techniques, as Jacques Ellul explains, are the totality of methods rationally organized to achieve maximum efficiency in every area of cultural activity. Techniques are what integrate machine technologies into society. In being based on rationality, they become independent of traditions governed by moral values not centered on achieving greater efficiency (1964, 3–22). Ellul goes on to explain that the uses of techniques are an integral part of science, which leads to the question of whether scientists understand how the uses of different techniques and, more specifically, how machine technologies introduce changes into the culture. The impact or cultural mediating characteristics of a technology, in turn, lead back to the questions about the Janus nature of the science driven uses of technologies (used here to include both techniques and machines).

The question can be reframed as: if the deep cultural assumptions that underlie the scientific method, and if the technologies relied upon by different sciences are not culturally neutral and are not an inherently progressive force, and if the scientist ignores the nature of the technologically driven cultural changes, can she/he be aware of when the intended progressive outcome of the new knowledge and research become a destructive force? These questions bring us to what should have been learned in the early stages of a scientist's education. Indeed, this should be learned by everyone if they are to take responsibility for the consequences that follow from the use of different technologies.

The twin myths of cultural neutrality and of being an inherently progressive force relieve people from taking responsibility for their actions. When their actions have a destructive impact on the life sustaining cultural and natural systems, the question about how to understand the cultural amplification and reduction characteristics of different technologies becomes extremely important. This is especially important if we are to recognize how scientists, when relying upon technologies such as print and the Internet, undermine the exercise of ecological intelligence. For example, when prior and current scientific knowledge, as well as current research findings and debates, are stored and communicated through the technology of the printed word, what is amplified are a number of misconceptions about the objective and factual nature of what appears in print—which in turn reinforces the deep cultural misconceptions that ignore the emergent, relational, and ethnocentric patterns of thinking. The conduit view of language that is reinforced in print-based storage, communication, and patterns of thinking, as mentioned earlier, also hides the metaphorical nature of language that carries forward earlier cultural conceptual templates that continue to guide current thinking. What the technology of print undermines is the awareness that facts and objective accounts encode human interpretations, including past misconceptions and silences.

The important and generally overlooked issue is how print and its supporting techniques amplify the abstract thinking of the Western elites who marginalized awareness of the face-to-face and emergent, relational, and co-dependent cultural and natural ecologies within which people live their everyday lives. Environmental scientists who understand the nature of ecological systems, rather than the fixed abstract world represented by mainstream Western philosophers, face a special challenge in communicating to a public socialized to think in terms of rigid categories, independent entities, either/or patterns of thinking, and an external world that needs to be brought under human control.

The technologies of print and data amplify the Cartesian model of intelligence where the individual is separate from the observed world that is to be rationally manipulated. Yet, even being socialized to this pattern of thinking does not preclude how ongoing changes in relationships and what is being communicated by the Other (both human and by natural systems) does not change a basic feature of everyday life: namely, exercising what can be called an individually centered ecological form of intelligence. The cultural and natural ecologies of everyday life (that is, the emergent, relational and co-dependent nature of life processes) need to be understood as involving networks or information pathways where the semiotic exchanges are responses to what Gregory Bateson referred to as the "differences which make a difference" that are the basic units in various biological and cultural semiotic processes. These differences that lead to a difference in the response of the Other, which may be the chemistry of a non-native plant that drives off pollinators, the tone of voice that communicates a lack of sincerity, the car that is speeding and weaving down the road, are the basic units of information that lead to a different response on the part of the Other. In short, everyone exercises a limited degree of ecological intelligence as they respond in culturally prescribed patterns to the messages communicated through the information pathways within the larger cultural and natural ecological systems within which they participate. The traffic light, and now the overhead revenue collecting camera, as well as the weather system making relationships and patterns at the intersection less visible, are all part of an ecology of information that alerts us to what is occurring in the emergent, relational, and co-dependent. Other ecologies of information (semiotic) exchanges to which we respond include the classroom, the office, the basketball court, the kitchen, the homeless living on the street, the corporate boardroom, and people living lives made redundant by computer systems.

The culturally derived interpretative framework may lack the vocabulary essential to recognizing the messages being communicated, which has the effect of limiting the exercise of ecological intelligence to the taken for granted thinking of others. As just suggested a limited form of ecological intelligence is exercised when driving an SUV that involves responding to the differences that make a difference in negotiating through traffic, including traffic lights and the behavior of other drivers and bike riders. Every cultural and natural context, ranging from an ongoing conversation to driving a car that has a huge carbon footprint, involves responding to the patterns that connect, but too often the individually centered exercise of ecological intelligence does not recognize the patterns that have ecological importance such as purchasing food that has to be flown from another part of the world. These are the differences that make a difference in terms of how life sustaining ecosystems are being impacted. A limited form of ecological intelligence is also exercised when "reading" ongoing changes occurring in the cultural and nature ecologies when pursuing an objective such as taking the children to a soccer match. But moving to a level of exercising ecological intelligence such as being aware that the amount of carbon dioxide being put into the atmosphere that contributes to the acidification of the world's oceans that will, in the immediate decades ahead, threaten the children's future prospects, is undermined by the cultural emphasis on individual self determination and the myth of individual intelligence.

The "I want" and "I need" mindset limits awareness of the connections between the higher than usual temperatures and the amount of gas being put into the tank of an SUV, resulting in the differences that are making a difference in terms of our future survival. Taken for granted outmoded cultural assumptions such as thinking of the world in mechanistic terms and of change as inherently progressive, as well as how the other aspects of the vocabulary handed down from the past, may still encode the misconceptions of earlier generations that limit awareness of what is being communicated through the information pathways that were not understood in the past. For example, the farmer who relies upon technologies such as genetically engineered seeds to increase crop yields, fertilizers and herbicides like Roundup, is less likely to be aware of what is being communicated within and between the interdependent ecological systems by the absence of birds and other creatures. My recent hour-drive through California's central valley in early October led to the number of insects collected on the front of the car to be no more than what could be counted on one hand. What are the life sustaining messages being communicated within the interdependent ecological systems that include a farming culture highly dependent upon the use of pesticides, the local bird populations, and other systems dependent upon a viable food web?

Another example of how the prejudices encoded in a taken for granted interpretative framework undermines awareness of the information being communicated within and between cultural and natural ecological systems can be seen in how Western science is upheld as the standard for judging the development of other cultures—which too often has led to ignoring the place-based in-depth knowledge that many indigenous culture have acquired, including their mathematics and systems of measurements. That their understanding of natural systems may be guided by moral/spiritual values is not seen as important—even though, in terms of the Quechua of the Peruvian Andes, they have developed one of the most diverse agricultural systems in the world. To reiterate a key point: the language and thus interpretive frameworks acquired in becoming socialized both illuminate and hide—with both being influenced by the taken for granted ways in which the language is acquired and continually reinforced.

A shared characteristic of cultural and natural ecologies is the complexity of the semiotic processes that sustain them—at the level of cells, the behavior of animals, and the metaphorical thinking encoded in interpersonal behavior and in the built environment. Exercising ecological intelligence requires giving close attention both to how and what is being communicated by the Other; and this includes being aware of past influences—as well as how one's own response influences future relationships. What separates the individually centered exercise of ecological intelligence from the long-term ecologically sustainable expressions of intelligence is the ability to discriminate between the patterns that are destructive and those that strengthen the self renewing capacity of cultural and natural systems. That is, this level of exercising ecological intelligence has a broader perspective that takes into account the current and future state of cultural and natural systems as well as the impacts on the plight of billions of people. It involves, first and foremost, the ability to carry out an essential step in the scientific method: namely, giving close attention to what is being communicated through the information pathways within the cultural and natural ecologies—that is, how it affects the behavior and future relationships with others, including the animals, plants, and other natural systems.

The Janus nature of science and technology can be seen more clearly when it is recognized that the technologies of print and digitization that scientists heavily promote amplify the long standing tradition in the West of privileging abstract thinking over what is learned from reliance upon place-based embodied experiences. Over reliance upon the surface and dated accounts reproduced in print-based cultural storage and communication, as well as in the even more abstract and limited representations encoded in data, marginalize what can be learned from the senses, personal and collective memories, historical knowledge, and ongoing communication within the cultural and natural ecologies. The latter are involved in being ecologically aware of the patterns and relationships that connect, and they provided a fuller understanding of the emergent, relational and co-dependent cultural and natural ecologies. The difference between reading about a person's craft knowledge and skill in making something, and actually observing—or more importantly, being physically, creatively, and mentally engaged in carrying out the task on one's own terms, is the difference between living in the limited world of abstractions and being fully involved in the multiple worlds of emergent relationships. This difference can be seen in what separates the experience of reading about a musical performance and actually playing within a group of musicians, between what separates the abstract reading a recipe and reliance upon all the senses required in orchestrating the multiple relationships in preparing a curry.

When the emergent, relational and co-dependent experiences are limited by what can be encoded in the technology of print, what gets represented is immediately dated. Print also provides only a surface knowledge which is, in turn, influenced by the taken for granted pattern of thinking of the writer. Printed accounts also are interpreted by readers whose own interpretative frameworks may further distort both the original event or the articulation of an idea, as well as the interpretation of the person who has provided the original written account. In effect, while print serves many useful purposes, it too often becomes a multi-layered ecology of misinterpretations that also hide that words are metaphors that have a history and, in too many instances, reproduce the misconceptions of earlier eras. Prime examples of these multi-layered ecologies of misinterpretations can be seen in how the writings of the major Western philosophers misrepresented the complexities of their own cultures—including the achievements of their cultural commons, as well as how the ideas of these philosophers have been interpreted by today's philosophy professors and social theorists as being relevant to promoting rational thought in cultures that are profoundly different from the cultures of the philosophers. And the students, sitting on the deck chairs of the modern Titanic they mistakenly assume to be a classroom, will find themselves unable to conceptualize alternatives to what will become a personal issue of survival as the pH factor of the world's oceans increases to life killing levels in the decades ahead, and as the rise of global temperatures set in motion other life threatening changes in the world's cultural and natural ecosystems.

In short, what print and data reduce is the interpersonal accountability that is often part of face-to-face communication. The people who construct the abstract representations found in print and now data too often experience personal gains without being held accountable. How do we hold Ayn Rand accountable for her Objectivist theory that promotes personal selfishness, and how do we hold accountable the computer scientists who have opened the floodgates for hackers to exploit the cultural systems that previously provided a modicum of privacy and security? The abstract systems created by earlier elites now serve the interests of the new elites that now control a major portion of the world's wealth—while at the same time promoting economic systems that are destroying the Earth's natural systems. Would the E. O. Wilsons, Richard Dawkins, and Ray Kurzweils within the scientific community maintain that this is in line with Darwin's prediction of how the environment determines which genes and memes are better adapted in a constantly changing environment? Is the "winner take all" mentality essentially what Herbert Spencer meant when he coined the phrase "survival of the fittest" to explain the workings of natural selection?

What is reduced or lost by the technologies of print and data is the dynamic complexity and place-based nature of the actual experience. The printed word is easily reified by readers—with the process of reification leading to a universal truth such as free markets, individual freedom, literacy being a sign of an advanced culture, and so forth. A major problem in the West is that an excessive and uncritical reliance upon print-based knowledge can lead to political and economic decisions based on abstract thinking that ignore the need to understand differences in local cultural contexts. A recent example is the hundreds of millions of dollars spent on creating for the tribal cultures of Afghanistan a Western legal system that is far less effective than the traditional tribal systems for settling disputes. The people continue to turn to these traditional systems rather to those based on Western assumptions. Imposing a Western model of democratic decision making in cultures that do not have the Western idea of an autonomous individual is a continuing problem. Unfortunately, the failures, such as MIT's Nicholas Negroponte's effort to provide every child in the world an inexpensive yet durable computer, regardless of the child's culture, has not led to rethinking the conceptual basis of foreign policies or why so many abstract ideas of Western philosophers and social theorists have become reified and are so ecologically problematic.

It was the abstract (that is, culturally uninformed) thinking of Western philosophers such as Plato, John Locke, Adam Smith, René Descartes, and Herbert Spencer, as well as more current abstract thinkers such as Ayn Rand and Milton Friedman that provided the abstract ideas and values that continue as the basis for thinking of such supposed universals as private property, free markets, a rational process free of historical/cultural influences, and the survival of the fittest—which have been the dominant ethos of market capitalism.

Digitizing the ecologies of the work place, consumer behaviors, communication with others, and print-based accounts of historical events also involves a loss of knowledge of local contexts. This loss, in turn, strengthens the ability of elites to use data as the basis for such decisions as replacing workers with robots and computer driven systems, and targeting people's consumer habits. The amplification and reduction characteristics of digital technologies, which scientists have largely ignored, include the following reductions: marginalizing the complexity and importance of local contexts, loss of intergenerational communication, privacy, security from hackers, historical knowledge essential to understanding what needs to be conserved and what needs to be changed, the loss of the world's linguistic diversity, yielding control over one's own life as personal data is sold to corporations and governmental agencies. What the digital revolution amplifies is efficiency, personal conveniences (and there are many), profits, centralized control in decision making—plus a score of now essential functions necessary to maintaining a modern infrastructure and in carrying out important research. These losses and gains reflect the Janus nature of digital technologies that computer scientists, as a group, associate with modern development and progress—while ignoring the traditions being overturned—including the intergenerational knowledge and skills essential to the cultural commons.

Unfortunately, the scientists promoting the globalizing of a digitally connected world, and envisioning super computers replacing humans in the process of evolution, are driven by a combination of libertarianism and market liberalism, and are not asking about the forms of local knowledge and skills, as well as patterns of moral reciprocity that are being lost as more thinking and communication are mediated by the amplification and reduction characteristics of the Internet. Their books are noteworthy for the lack of awareness of the important differences that separate face-to-face intergenerationally connected communities from digitally connected communities that promote the form of individual autonomy that serves the interests of the market system (Stock, 1993; Schmidt and Cohen, 2013; Kurzweil, 1999, 2005, 2012; Dyson, 1998; Drexler, 2013). The grass roots localism movement now spreading to different regions of the world represents an important shift away from the consumer/industrial/individualistic culture that is still promoted by the digital revolution. It is important to note that the localism movement involves place-based face-to-face and intergenerational communication as well as mentoring—which are undermined by the digital revolution.

There is another aspect of modern culture that indicates a lack of moral clarity on the part of many scientists. That is, whose political and economic agenda will they align themselves with by providing the basic research and technologies that will enable these groups to achieve their primary agendas? Where in the education of scientists do they learn about the differences between ideologies, and the record of how the moral systems encoded in these ideologies have impacted both humans and natural systems? The record of non-Jewish scientists working to perpetuate the myth-driven politics of Nazi Germany raises serious questions about how the scientific method fosters a taken for granted attitude toward equating scientific research with progress—regardless of whether it serves the economic interests of Monsanto, the pharmaceutical industry, the defense industry, or the current myth of entering the post-biological phase of evolution. Every ideology, including that of Germany's National Socialism, is based on deep cultural assumptions about what constitute moral and immoral behavior, and scientists cannot claim to operate outside of cultural relationships that are never value neutral.

People socialized to take for granted the conduit view of language, which hides that words (iconic and the root metaphors that provide the interpretative frameworks) are less likely to recognize that a culture's moral values are often encoded in the analogs that frame the meaning of words such as "progress," "weeds," "natural resources," and so forth. The analogs, which reflect the thinking of earlier eras, sanction certain behaviors over others as being moral. The early guidelines for the scientific method, with its emphasis on observing, measuring, and predicting behaviors in the observable world, excluded moral issues as being a legitimate concern of scientists. These guidelines, which can be better understood as an ideology, were established during a period in Western thinking when there was no understanding of how the metaphorical nature of language encodes the moral codes of the people who succeeded in establishing the analogs that framed the meaning of words such as "illiterate," "primitive," "wasteland," "natural selection," and "experimentation."

That the above vocabulary legitimated behaviors that some now regard as immoral is yet another example of how the naming of patterns brings awareness to what was previously ignored. The above examples of Western moral biases encoded in a metaphorical language handed down from the past also bring out how differences in moral codes are influenced by the mythopoetic narratives of the culture—which often involve spiritual/linguistic ecologies that are beyond what can be understood by the limited forms of knowledge allowed by the scientific method. Attacks on traditional religions by scientists such as E. O. Wilson, Richard Dawkins, and Francis Crick argue that religions are based on outdated memes, and now must be replaced by the rational process that does not stray beyond the empirical evidence. Carl Sagan summed up in the following way why science rather than religions should guide human actions:

> Think of how many religions attempt to validate themselves with prophecy. Think of how many people rely on these prophecies however vague, however unfulfilled, to support or prop up their beliefs. Yet has there ever been a religion with the *prophetic accuracy and reliability of science*? There isn't a religion on this planet that doesn't long for a comparable ability—precise

and repeatedly demonstrated before committed skeptics—to foretell future events. No other human institution comes close.

(1997, 33, italics added)

This categorical statement comes after Sagan claims that science and spirituality should not be seen as mutually exclusive. But spirituality, as Wilson also holds, must not rely upon ways of knowing that cannot be validated by science's insistence upon observable and measurable evidence.

The mix of individual self direction in matters of what constitutes moral relationships with others and with the natural environment, when combined with the new meta-narrative of Darwin's theory of natural selection now being given an ontological status by many scientists, would not be so problematic if we were living in a robust and self-renewing environment. Unfortunately, this is no longer the case. Thus, it is imperative that scientists have an understanding of the diversity of the world's religions rather than dismissing them based on their own narrow experience with various interpretations of Christianity, Judaism, and Islam (especially their more fundamentalist beliefs and practices).

In many instances, culture, spirituality, and religion are inseparable, such as the mythopoetic narratives of the Hopi, the Quechua of the Peruvian Andes, and hundreds of other indigenous cultures—including the Aboriginal cultures of Australia. These religions, if they can be called that, carry forward generations of knowledge of how to live in morally responsible relationships with each other and with the environment—including the other-than-human-world. Even the dominant Western religions that have tendencies that promote violence toward others and the environment, have important moral guidelines that are increasingly difficult to live by—given the hyper-materialistic world these religions helped create.

The point is that if we consider the Eightfold Path of Buddhism we find an emphasis on living in accordance with traditions that have been practiced for thousands of years—and not on declarations about the importance of the subjective judgments of individuals who increasingly are living in the abstract and violent world created by computer programmers. The Eightfold Path, which could serve as the guidelines for sustainable living in the West's increasingly stressed environment, include: (1) Right Views; (2) Right Intent; (3) Right Speech; (4) Right Conduct; (5) Right Livelihood; (6) Right Effort; (7) Right Mindfulness; (8) Right Concentration (Smith, 1991, 106–113). Following the Eightfold Path of Buddhism is not easy as it requires avoiding the distractions of the material world, the shifting views and reward systems of others, and may lead to a level of spirituality that cannot be tested or explained by what meets the scientists' standards for empirical verification. If we were to identify the Eightfold Path upheld in the West it would include: (1) Pursue self interest; (2) Achieve greater self autonomy; (3) Own as much property as possible; (4) Create your own knowledge and values; (5) Support the market system; (6) View traditions as sources of backwardness; (7) Promote new technologies and development of markets; (8) Recognize your divine right to consume as much of the world's resources as possible.

While environmental scientists would find problematic aspects of the Eightfold Path for guiding the thinking and behavior in the West, neither they nor their colleagues working to advance the economic agendas of environmentally destructive corporations such as Monsanto and Dow Chemical—and the culturally destructive agendas of the major players promoting the digital revolution—have provided anything in the way of understanding how to question the assumptions underlying the West's dominant moral ethos. Nor have they suggested viable alternatives. Ironically, the emerging localism movement as well as the cultural commons that are still passed forward through face-to-face and mentoring relationships in every community exhibit values more in line with those of Buddhism and Confucianism (minus Confucianism's support of right relationships within a rigid status system).

Confucianism also does not fit the view of religion held by Wilson, Dawkins, Crick, and Sagan, as well as many other scientists who are proposing that evolution become the new meta-narrative that should guide human behavior. Education that promotes Confucius' insights of how to live with others, including the environment, includes emphasizing the inner development of the person that, in turn, leads to less competitive, stressful, and hubris driven relationships with others: (1) **Jen** which promotes humility toward others and respect for oneself. (2) **Chun tzu** leads to what Martin Buber refers to as the I-Thou relationships that makes the other fully present in a non-exploitive way—that is, the person of Chun tzu is the opposite of the petty and mean person that uses the Other to meet a personal need. (3) **Li** refers to propriety in relationships, which also requires the proper use of language in naming relationships—with both being guided by a sense of harmony and proper balance. (4) **Te** refers to the exercise of power that promotes trust among the people, and between the people and government. (5) **Wen** is achieved through valuing and practicing the arts—which attracts others rather than engendering fear and envy that lead to conflicts (Smith, 1991, 178–180).

Of course these guides for living in peaceful relationships with others have been transformed by other cultural traditions in ways that serve the interests of the politically and economically powerful. The important question is, given the argument in the West that Darwin's narrative of natural selection should replace all religions that do not adhere to the scientists' strict empirical standards, should religions that do not promote the exploitation of the environment and other people be taken seriously. And if scientists promote their disappearance by globalizing the Western digital technologies and the values of the market place that alienates youth from the oral traditions of their culture, will they be able to lead youth to adopt similar non-violent pathways of existing in an increasingly crowded world that is facing the real prospects of what is being called the "sixth extinction" (Kolbert, 2014)?

Max Weber (1864–1920), the noted German sociologist, identified a fundamental difference between Asian religions and the dominant religions in the West. That is, he noted that the religions of Buddhism and Confucianism took an exemplary approach to attracting followers, while in the West the dominant approach exhibited by religions, its capitalist economic system, its science, and its educational institutions have been strongly messianic. Perhaps the best and most problematic example of the messianic drive to convert other cultures to its increasingly reductive approach to knowledge and to new forms of economic dependency is the digital revolution that leading computer scientists justify on the grounds that the world is entering the post-biological phase dictated by the evolutionary process that has guided the world since the Big Bang. While the diversity of Western religions are partly responsible for the myths that supported the economic systems that are putting at risk the future of life itself, some of their narratives have carried forward the wisdom about sustainable and morally accountable human relationships, as well as the dangers of hubris and an excessive focus on materialistic values. The question that the next generation of scientists must confront is how to locate the sources of wisdom that warn against the many expressions of hubris in the sciences and in the corporations that still rely upon the myth of progress still rooted in the even deeper myth that promotes the pursuit of self-interest.

The lack of clear and compelling guidelines that establish the boundaries between science and scientism, and excludes moral issues as a legitimate concern of scientists, relieves scientists from considering the moral issues surrounding the development of toxic chemicals, the military uses of robots, and, now, the surveillance systems that are taking us down the slippery slope leading to the merging of the corporate, military, and ideologically driven alliance that created the state of perpetual warfare similar to what happened in fascist Germany.

However, not all scientists ignore the moral issues that arise in the emerging, relational, and co-dependent world we live in. Environmental scientists are very clear about the moral issues related to conserving habitats and species. Indeed, from the beginning of the 19th century they have supported genuine forms of conservatism, which was expressed in the political actions of various conservation groups. Their early thinking corresponded to the political and cultural conservatism of Edmund Burke, T.S. Eliot, and Michael Oakeshott—and to the current thinking of writers such as Wendell Berry and Vandana Shiva. The important question is, given the narrow education of most scientists: How many scientists are aware of the Orwellian language that now leads to calling market liberals and libertarians conservatives when their primary agenda is to promote the globalization of free markets, the Western idea (and myth) of the autonomous individual, and the economic exploitation of the environment? These ideologies encode moral agendas that affect the most fundamental relationships and prospects for meeting basic human needs. And how many scientists are aware of earlier and present interpretations of Darwin's theory that have given legitimacy to the market liberals that exploited both people and the environment in order to expand markets and profits? Where are the scientists who are raising questions about how scientists such as E. O. Wilson and Richard Dawkins, as well as computer scientists such as Ray Kurzweil, are explaining cultural achievements as expressions of natural selection? If Darwin's theory is open to different interpretations that replicate the Social Darwinism of the last century that was reduced to slogans such as "survival of the fittest," and if scientists continue to take for granted the root metaphors of progress, individualism, and a mechanistic world, is there a real possibility that scientists will recognize how they are complicit in furthering the corporate mindset and values that are destroying the natural systems we depend upon?

As the corporate and political leaders of the country are again viewing the nation as falling behind in the technological and economic race to exploit what remains of the Earth's natural resources, educators are being asked to narrow the educational priorities to what will grow the economy, and to what can be tested by computers. Like in previous eras of national peril, the sciences, mathematics, engineering, and technologies are to be given special priorities. It is important to note that the previous Cold War era efforts to strengthen student competencies in these areas did not lead to a profession of scientists, engineers, and technologists who possessed a deep knowledge of their own culture as well as that of other cultures—or to a knowledge of the cultural traditions that have a less destructive impact on natural systems.

One of the ironies of globalizing Western technologies, especially digital technologies, is that the groups resisting the loss of their cultural traditions now have access to more lethal weapons, and can strike deep into the dominant cultures in ways that were impossible before. The generations of scientists, engineers, and technologists educated in the Cold War era, which set the standards for the following generations, were educated to view their highly specialized knowledge and technological skills as the most advanced in the world, and like the globalizing agenda of the early and current Christian missionaries and corporate heads, their task was to spread the Western mathematics, sciences, engineering, and technological prowess throughout the world. The failure of this mindset can be seen in how these colonizing efforts are being rejected in Muslim cultures, as well as by the growing resistance within the indigenous cultures that make up a significant percentage of the world's population.

This latest effort to tie educational reforms to what corporate leaders and the politicians think is essential to expanding the consumer economy into every region of the world now goes by the label of the Common Core Curriculum. It is being promoted by using the time-tested techniques of the advertising world: namely, using the words that are like comfort food to the non-reflective public to sell poor quality and largely unneeded products. As it works nearly every time, the Common Core Curriculum is being sold the same way. The promise is that it will prepare students for life and careers in the 21st century and for college—which will lead to rising higher on the pyramid of consumerism that is the ultimate measure of personal success. Not mentioned are the efforts to create computer systems and robots that will displace workers—including classroom teachers and university professors as online education creates more profits for those who own the digital systems and can be easily tailored to what parents want their children to learn.

The STEM part of the Common Core educational reform may represent the last generation that can possibly make a difference before the "survival of the fittest" mentality spreads like a virus in response to the even more extreme changes in natural systems that lie immediately ahead. The slow and increasingly ineffective process we call democracy may have only a few decades before the world enters the endgame of armed struggle to control resources and populations—which means that the STEM-based educational reforms will also be limited in terms of making a positive contribution. The rate at which the chemistry and temperatures of the world's oceans are changing, as well as the extreme shifts in weather patterns—which will only become more extreme when the vast quantities of methane gases are released as the Arctic warms—need to be taken into account if we are to introduce educational reforms that avoid the mistakes of previous efforts. The consensus among scientists is that the world may have 50 or so years to make a difference—which means students in the early grades could still be living as the world enters the coming era of mass social chaos. This 50 or so years prediction holds for when potable water will be too limited to meet worldwide demand, when the acidification of the world's oceans devastate needed sources of protein, and when the warming of the Arctic is likely to release trapped methane gas that could raise the world's temperature by 5 to 6 degrees Celsius—which will spell the end of life as we know it.

That the teachers and professors who will be involved in developing the new STEM curriculum were mostly educated in the last decades of the 20th century suggests that the prospects of addressing the silences and misconceptions that were passed forward in educating the previous generation of scientists and technologists are not good. In spite of all the lofty rhetoric about progress, cultural lag is real. And what is learned in public schools and universities is a powerful reason for the cultural lag that occurs at the deepest levels of the culture's dominant belief system. Public schools and universities still pass forward the assumptions taken for granted by the elites of previous generations who were unaware of environmental limits and who did not understand the emergent, relational, and co-dependent world we live in. Nor did they understand the nature and ecological importance of the world's diversity of cultural commons that represented the largely non-monetized traditions that are now undergoing a revitalization under the name of the localism movement.

In the next chapter I will provide an explanation of how the aspects of culture identified here as missing in the education of the current generation of scientists and technologists can be introduced to the next and perhaps last generation of scientists and technologists. I understand that the digital revolution has shortened attention spans, and has created the expectation that the surface knowledge encoded in print and data is an adequate basis for making decisions. But what is the alternative to promoting the possibility of constructive changes held out by the Janus nature of critical and culturally informed thinking?

5

EDUCATING THE NEXT AND PERHAPS LAST GENERATION OF SCIENTISTS AND TECHNOLOGISTS

The major concern that prompted Bill Gates, Rex Tillerson (CEO of Exxon Mobil) and the heads of major corporations to support the Common Core Curriculum reforms is that America is falling behind in the education of scientists and engineers. Those who have received their marching orders from corporations and from the politicians bought by corporations have succeeded in establishing a new set of national priorities: namely, to encourage more women and ethnic minorities to join the ranks of scientists and engineers and thus to position themselves for a lifetime of higher paying jobs. This is compared with the number of white males working in these two fields, which was 51 percent in 2013, with only 20 percent being white women—with the percentages falling off the charts for Hispanic and African American males and females. The concern about aligning the reforms in STEM (science, technology, engineering, and mathematics) with unresolved social justice issues is an important step forward. But it falls short of addressing whether the new STEM graduates will be able to avoid the mistakes of Americans who brought their Western science/engineering/technology perspective to the task of building the new infrastructures that would reverse the gains of the insurgents in Iraq, Afghanistan, and other Muslim cultures. The key point is not that of assessing the strengths and weaknesses of Western inspired development programs, but the educational reforms that supposedly lead to a more equitable ethnic and gender mix of graduates. Are current STEM programs adequately informed that the globally connected world we now live in requires more than a surface understanding of different cultures—as well as key characteristics that are shared by all cultures?

Pure scientific research will be the focus of only a minority of STEM graduates, with the majority working for governments, corporations, various sectors within military, and NGOs that will become increasingly important in the years ahead as the deepening ecological crisis leads to more military conflicts and to more people becoming homeless and destitute.

The critical question is where to begin in engaging these future STEM students in an understanding of the deep and largely overlooked characteristics of the cultural and natural ecologies that influence their sense of identities, taken for granted behaviors, values, and what they are unaware of. In short the critical question is: what do STEM graduates need to understand about cultures, their own as well as other cultures, in order to avoid perpetuating the scientism that has accompanied the well meaning but uninformed efforts of many leading scientists? What follows are the initial understandings that can be gained as the classroom teachers or others provide the vocabulary that enables the taken for granted cultural patterns to become the focus of the students' awareness of the emergent and relational world in which they live.

In addition to identifying aspects of the student's otherwise taken for granted cultural experiences, examples of how the lack of understanding has led to mistakes in the thinking of previous generations of scientists, technologists and engineers also need to be discussed. Two important themes will be constantly kept in focus: (1) that the uses of science, technology, and engineering cannot be divorced from cultural issues. And (2) that learning to rely upon the scientific method in observing cultural patterns (including those taken for granted by the observer—which is the harder task) is as important as using the scientific method to learn about the natural world.

In order to overcome the silences about cultural issues that have been missing in the education of the current generation of scientists, technologists, engineers, and mathematicians—as well as be useful at all levels of the STEM curriculum— what follows will be a series of categories of culture such as the nature of taken for granted ways of thinking and the cultural commons, a brief explanation of the importance of these categories, and a series of questions that will help ground students' understandings. The latter will encourage students to think beyond the applied and often narrowly focused problem solving approaches in science, technology, engineering, and mathematics, and thus to develop the habit of situating their problem solving skills within the larger context of cultural differences in addressing the daily ecologically unsustainable practices. As noted earlier, ignorance of cultural issues that leads to scientism and to colonizing developmental projects—including promoting Western technologies—not only undermines local traditions that have a smaller ecological footprint, but also contributes to the spread of international violence. The starting place for introducing students in STEM programs to what should have been learned in public schools and universities is how to understand the different uses of the word culture within the sciences. But more important is understanding the traditions, beliefs, daily practices, and linguistic patterns that vary from culture to culture—and that now should be understood as cultural ecologies.

Scientific Uses of the World "Culture"

Different areas of scientific research rely upon the world "culture" but it is usually understood in a narrow and limited way dictated by the scientific method. The most prominent is its use as a verb; that is, the cultivation of microorganisms such as bacteria and tissues in a controlled medium. In various labs, the word culture will also be used in the context of referring to an experimental procedure and outcome. It is used more in the field of biology and in the context of a controlled experiment. The word culture is notably absent in the fields of neuroscience and technology (especially computer science) as it introduces different symbolic issues that threaten the narrow and even ideologically driven interpretative frameworks of these fields of inquiry. An anthropology/linguistic understanding of what the word culture encompasses would undermine the certainty that accompanies reducing mental activities to what can be observed on an MRI screen. And this broader understanding of cultures as involving different ways of knowing would force computer scientists to acknowledge that reducing human experience to data, which cannot account for the ongoing historical/cultural influences on human experience, involves a fundamental transformation of people's lives—including the loss of ecologically sustainable and social justice traditions.

Scientists that have adopted interpretative frameworks that focus on the emergent, relational, and co-dependent nature of plants and animals may use the words ecologies and cultures as nearly interchangeable words. Archeologists and paleontologists rely upon an expanded understanding of what the word culture encompasses and thus provide explanations of cultural phenomena that cannot always be scientifically (that is, empirically) verified.

Questions for Students to Consider

1   Does the word culture have a universal meaning, or does the interpretative framework and research/problem solving agenda of the scientist, technologist, engineer, and mathematician frame how the meaning of the word is understood?
2   Do different understandings of the meaning of a word such as culture have political implications? What are some examples of how accepting the definition that prevails within one of the sciences, such as cognitive science and economics (if the latter can legitimately be called a science) disadvantages other groups and cultures?
3   If words are a human and thus cultural construction, how can we understand when they are used in ways that contribute to the well-being of others and when they serve the self interest of a social group?
4   Is it possible to identify examples of words that are politically neutral?

Importance of Taken for Granted Cultural Patterns

One of the reasons that scientists in a variety of fields, as well as many of the general public, do not have a deep understanding of their own culture, as well as other cultures, is that communication with others, including the patterns of communication in classrooms, on computer screens, and in the media generally, is what people are explicitly aware of and talk about with others. That is, people seldom engage in conversations that make explicit their taken for granted beliefs and values; indeed, what they take for granted largely sets the conceptual and conversational boundaries. This pattern is reinforced by parents and others, as well as by the formal educational process where what is tested is the students' explicit knowledge. Less noticed are what can be referred to as the taken for granted, implicit, and tacit knowledge and cultural patterns that represent the major stock of knowledge that is seldom considered. In short, what is taken for granted influences thinking and behaviors in ways that lie below the level of explicit awareness.

Taken for granted patterns of thinking handed down from the past include, within the dominant Western culture, thinking of traditions as sources of backwardness, progress as linear and leading to a brighter future, and technology as a neutral tool and as the latest expression of progress. Other cultures have their own taken for granted beliefs and practices, and because of their taken for granted status they frame what people take to be real and normal—and thus not as unique to their group.

As we can see in how long it took to recognize the bias and silences that characterized taken for granted patterns of gender and racial discrimination, as well as the beliefs about thinking of the environment as an endlessly exploitable resource—and the growing belief that science is free of biases and thus the most reliable guide to genuine human progress, it is important for future scientists, technologists, engineers, and mathematicians to be aware both of their own taken for granted patterns of thinking as well as the patterns of other cultures. What often limits awareness of the taken for granted beliefs and practices, including the silences carried forward from the past that also go unrecognized, is a lack of understanding of the role of language in carrying forward the stock of taken for granted knowledge, the history and economic advantageous of expert knowledge and practice that would be undermined if the taken for granted assumptions, use of language, and so forth, were to be made explicit.

Here are several taken for granted patterns of thinking held by scientists and technologists. The question is, what is taken for granted and what is being ignored?

> Technology is a resource-liberating mechanism. It can make the once scarce the now abundant.
>
> (Diamandis and Kotler, 2012, 4)

The language of the brain is based on neurons. To understand the brain you must understand neurons and especially how vast numbers of them act in parallel.

(Crick, 1994, 256, italics in the original)

Science for its part will test relentlessly every assumption about the human condition and in time uncover the bedrock of the moral and religious sentiments.

(Wilson, 1998, 265)

Questions for Students to Consider

1   Ask students to identify values and patterns of thinking and behavior that were taken for granted by previous generations such as how women and minorities were viewed. What are examples of taken for granted cultural patterns in other areas of every day life?

2   What cultural processes led to these taken for granted patterns of thinking, values, and relationships being made explicit? For example, was personal privacy taken for granted before the digital revolution? What taken for granted ways of thinking led to the loss of privacy being viewed as a progressive step forward? Can you list a number of taken for granted patterns of thinking that influenced peoples' behaviors toward the environment? Toward other cultural groups?

   Is the widely held view that technological innovations are expressions of progress, and that they should be globalized, an example of taken for granted thinking?

3   Given the examples of taken for granted patterns of thinking you have identified, how does what is taken for granted limit awareness of other relationships and possibilities? Start with an obvious example: how did taken for granted thinking about the ability of women limit their prospects? Do the taken for granted assumptions about progress and the role of science and technology in perpetuating it lead to ignoring the evidence of changes in the earth's ecosystems that may be beyond the abilities of science and technology to reverse?

In discussing the following characteristics of culture keep in mind that all of them may be partially or totally taken for granted. To reiterate an important point, we are not explicitly aware of most of our cultural patterns that are carried forward from the past—including the idea that we are autonomous thinkers and that we are continually replacing traditions with new ideas, values, and technologies.

The Language, Culture, Thought Connection: Or Why Objective Knowledge and Data are Modern Myths

It is important for students, regardless of their level of engagement in STEM curricula, to understand a number of misconceptions about language that continue to push even the most acclaimed scientists to drift into the realm of scientism with claims that bring the larger agenda of scientific inquiry into question. Essential to understanding how we think and communicate about our internal experiences as well as how we understand the world that is the focus of scientific inquiry is that words do not represent aspects of the world that we mistakenly refer to as facts, objective knowledge, and data. That is, there is no objective knowledge and ideas, just as there are now objective information and data. What we represent in terms of the vocabularies we acquire in becoming members of the larger language community are interpretations which may vary widely, depending upon the culture. That is, if facts, data, information, ideas, knowledge are dependent upon the use of language, they are all interpretations that reflect the taken for granted assumptions and meanings that were framed by the analogues settled upon in earlier time. What are mistakenly taken to be objective facts and data for most speakers of English encode a whole set of cultural assumptions about this being a human-centered world, the individual as being an external observer and autonomous thinker, and that words are not metaphors with a cultural history but provide an accurate and thus objective account of what they name. Language, not only reproduces earlier cultural pattern of interpretations, but also the moral codes that represent earlier stages of cultural development. For example, the metaphor of "women" reproduced over the centuries the moral codes for judging their behavior, potential in life, and where they ranked in the culture's status systems. Similarly, the metaphor "weed" also encodes what constitutes moral behavior toward its existence—that is, it is moral to exterminate it with a pesticide. Given the hidden influences on what are taken to be the meaning of words, they lead to interpretations that may be based on old superstitions and myths that do not take account of careful and systematic observations of the cultural and natural patterns that connect. Other interpretations, such as those of environmental scientists who are challenging the more widely held myth of endless progress, will hold up under careful observations and critical scrutiny—but never represent a final Truth.

The reason that scientists, technologists, engineers, and mathematicians have so often misrepresented the world we live in is that they were educated, like the general public, to think of language as a conduit. That is, as a sender/receiver process whereby ideas, data, information, facts, and so forth can be communicated to others. This sender/receiver view of communication has the effect of hiding that most words are metaphors, which leads, in turn, to the idea that words represent an objective reality. An example of how both E. O. Wilson's taken for granted interpretive framework, as well as his ignoring that most words are metaphors, can be seen in the following explanation:

> Today, the greatest divide within humanity is not between races, or religions, or even, as widely believed, between the literate and illiterate. It is the chasm that separates scientific from prescientific cultures: Without the instruments and accumulated knowledge of the natural sciences—physics, chemistry, and biology—humans are trapped in a cognitive prison.
>
> (Wilson, 1998, 45)

It reads like an objective account of historical developments, but it is actually his interpretation that is based on a number of unexamined assumptions—including how branches of contemporary science such as computer science and neuroscience exclude other ways of thinking—which can also be understood as a cognitive prison.

Nearly all the words in Wilson's quotation are metaphors. That is, the meaning of words such as "greatest," "divide," "races," "instruments," "natural," "trapped," "cognitive," "prison" have been framed by the analogs settled upon at an earlier time in the culture's history. The initial understanding of the new, such as what do we mean by "trapped," or "cognitive" involves relying upon a previous experience, idea, and use of words whose meaning are already established as the analog for understanding what is new—such as "divide" and "cognitive prison." All the words in Wilson's statement have a history, and their meanings, as Wilson uses them, reproduce the analogs settled upon at an earlier time in the culture's history. That is, metaphors such as literate and illiterate reproduce an earlier established pattern of either/or thinking, as well as the prejudice that represents literate as a more advanced state of consciousness than an illiterate (or an oral) level of consciousness.

Carl Sagan's statement about giving the highest rewards to disproving "established beliefs" is yet another example of how words (metaphors) encode the analogs that reflect the prejudices and misconceptions of earlier eras. In the case of Sagan's reference to established beliefs, he is clearly reproducing the Enlightenment thinker's misconceptions about established beliefs—which were associated with the superstitions of the feudal era, and not with the wide variety of craft knowledge, skills, and technologies used to build the beautiful cathedrals and to sustain daily life within their largely non-monetized cultural commons.

To summarize what is often overlooked, especially when it is assumed the words refer to real events, ideas, processes, and that they can be used to communicate objective knowledge: most words are metaphors whose meanings were framed by the analogs settled upon in the past, and are being carried forward in the taken for granted process of socialization to how to think within the possibilities and limits of the inherited vocabulary. In effect, current patterns of thinking which involve individual perspectives and even the individual's misunderstandings also reproduce earlier expressions of intelligence—which includes the misconceptions, prejudices, genuine insights, and silences. Wilson's statement about how people were locked in a cognitive prison before the rise of Western science overlooks the depth of knowledge of the early Chinese, Muslim, as well as indigenous cultures in other parts of the world. Wilson's unrecognized cultural assumption about a linear form of progress in scientific and technological knowledge overlooks that, in addition to its genuine gains, Western science has also produced more lethal weapons, poisoned the environment with toxic chemicals, and has produced elite groups of scientists who are changing the world in ways that advance the interests of corporate capitalism.

Questions for Students to Consider

1   After students have examined how new ideas and the use of language are explained by the use of analogs where the new is understood in terms of what is already familiar (examples can be found in textbooks or in Google explanations), ask them to explain the process of analogic thinking to someone else. Several examples may prompt students to recognize other examples of how analogs frame the meaning of words such as the elementary textbook explanation of how disease is passed suggests that students think of disease as being passed in the same way they pass a ball to others. Another example is how a crop of vegetables was used as the analog for understanding silvaculture as a "crop" of trees. The metaphor used to understand the danger of countries falling to communism was likened to the behavior of dominos which set off a chain of events that can be predicted. Other examples of analogs that frame the meaning of metaphors such as Big Bang, Dark Matter, Strings, and so forth should also be discussed. If students cannot explain how the choice of analogs frames the meaning of words by using current examples, they do not really understand the political process of how the meaning of words become part of the Other's taken for granted way of thinking.

2   Ask students to consider the political implications of why certain groups were able to get their analogs accepted as framing the meaning of such words as "traditions," "data", "progress", "literate," and so forth. Discussing this process will bring out the political nature of language: namely, whose way of thinking will lead to controlling the thinking of others.

3   In order for students to recognize that the metaphorical nature of words encode earlier forms of intelligence (that is, ways of thinking based on culturally specific misconceptions, prejudices, insights, and silences), ask them to investigate how the analogs that framed the meaning of such words

as "woman," "nature," "individualism," "property," "corporation," and "ecology" have changed over time.

The important concept for students to understand is that words (metaphors) have a specific cultural history—which means that interpretations are also culturally influenced.

The Nature and Role of Root Metaphors

Root metaphors perform that same way as a culture's mythopoetic narratives, such as found in the *Book of Genesis*, Spider-Woman (Na'ashjéii asdzáá) in the Hopi culture, and Pachamama in Quechua culture. Every culture has its stories of origins that include explanations of how to live, where they came from and what the future holds if they fall short of what the creative force expects of them. These narratives provide the deep explanatory frameworks that are the basis of how everyday life is be interpreted. Several of the most powerful root metaphors in the West have been derived from earlier interpretations of the patriarchal and anthropocentric myths contained in the *Book of Genesis*. Other root metaphors in the West that provide the largely taken for granted interpretative frameworks include individualism, progress, mechanism, economism, evolution, and ecology. The origins of these culturally specific root metaphors can be traced to earlier narratives such as the *Book of Genesis* (patriarchy and a human-centered world), to events such as the use of the clock to organize the routines of daily life and the rise of modern science (mechanism), Enlightenment thinking (individualism), the rise of literacy and gains from modern science (progress), the Industrial Revolution (economism), the hegemony of the scientific paradigm (evolution), and the awareness of the misconceptions about human/nature relationships in these earlier root metaphors (ecology).

As the earlier example of the history of the root metaphor of mechanism demonstrates (see Chapter 2) the vocabulary that serves as the taken for granted interpretive framework becomes the basis for thinking about a wide range of cultural practices over a long period of the culture's history. For example, the language derived from thinking of the world as a mechanical process influenced the fields of politics, medicine, education, the creative process, and the sciences— which now includes digital technologies. What is often misunderstood because of the popular myth that individuals are autonomous thinkers, capable of having *their own* ideas about all aspects of life, is that the vocabularies we inherit from the past, such as the vocabularies influenced by the root metaphors of individualism, progress, mechanism, and economism (which support each other as a metainterpretative framework) not only frame how life processes are interpreted, but exclude other possibilities. They limit awareness of other possibilities by virtue of excluding the necessary vocabularies for naming and understanding different relationships.

In effect, words, and collectively as interpretive frameworks based on different root metaphors, both illuminate and hide. For example, the vocabulary that supports the root metaphor of mechanism lacks the words for accurately understanding organic processes, for understanding the importance of wisdom, and for understanding the cultural roots of the metaphorical language that influences taken for granted patterns of thinking. The evidence for this generalization can be checked out by examining whether the fields of neuroscience and computer science recognize differences in cultural ways of knowing, and the influence of a culture's different languaging processes on human thought and embodied experiences. For example, do the root metaphors that neuroscientists take for granted (mechanism, individualism, progress) allow them to consider how a noun-dominated English language influences consciousness differently than one that relies more on the use of verbs, such as the Ojibway and the Cree First Nations of Canada? How do these scientists explain the semiotic pathways that connect all participants in both cultural and natural ecologies, and which should be understood as ecologies of primitive and complex responses to the difference which make a difference in the emergent and relational world? Does the intelligence of the architect and craft people that is encoded in the building I walk by or enter continue to communicate in ways that affect my thinking, aesthetic awareness, and behavior? Does animal behavior express the exercise of intelligence—though of a different kind? Or does intelligence only exist if it is expressed in the behavior of neurons that can be mapped by an MRI scan? And what does the scan of the neurons tell us about the cultural influences on behaviors, ideas, and values that are the expressions of intelligence?

Questions for Students to Consider

1   Ask the students to identify the root metaphors that frame the thinking in the following statements:

> SimEarth can be played in two modes, game and experimental. In game mode, you will try to develop, manage, and preserve your planet within allotted energy budgets.
>
> Muscles are engines which, like the steam engine and the internal combustion, use energy stored in chemical fuel to generate mechanical movement.
>
> (Dawkins, 1976, 47)

> What we call meaning is the linkage among neural networks created by the spreading excitation that enlarges imagery and engages emotions.
>
> (Wilson, 1998, 115)

> So what's left for humans? In one future, society takes a turn for the Luddite. We take Bill Joy's advice, follow the designs of the slow

food movement, and begin to backtrack with the Amish. . . . In the second, the majority of humanity will end up merging with technology, enhancing themselves both physically and cognitively.

(Diamandis and Kotler, 2012, 302–303)

To understand the brain, it is important to grasp that it is the end product of a long process of natural selection.

(Crick, 1994, 10)

Subjectivity is your private experience of the world. . . . It is just as real as the objective physical world.

(Gelernter, 2014, 19)

When we finally hit the fateful day when robots are smarter than us, not only will we no longer be the most intelligent being on earth, but our creations may make copies of themselves that are even smarter than they are. This army of self-replicating robots will then create endless future generations of robots, each one smarter than the previous ones.

(Kaku, 2011, 101)

2   Do any of these statements take account of cultural and linguistic influences on human intelligence and behaviors? Do they recognize that an uncritical way of thinking about progress has led to the introduction of vast quantities of toxic chemicals, to the loss of craft knowledge and even work opportunities, to the loss of privacy, and to techniques for manipulating consciousness? Does taking the root metaphor of progress for granted lead to ignoring that new ideas and innovations often have destructive consequences?

3   Do Western scientists have the right to dictate the changes that other cultures are to undergo? Is there an assumption that Western science and technology represent the most advanced form of knowledge—that is, the leading edge of progress?

4   Do the vocabularies in the above quotes reflect the influence of different root metaphors that provide the conceptual basis for thinking about the cultural roots of the ecological crisis? Do any of the above quotes suggest that living ecologically sustainable lives requires the guidance of wisdom? And where does wisdom come from?

5   An activity that will strengthen awareness of how the vocabularies of different root metaphors, which are themselves metaphors whose meanings were framed by the acceptance of analogs settled upon in earlier eras, provide useful interpretative frameworks within certain contexts but are limiting in terms of other contexts, can be achieved by having students identify the vocabularies that support different root metaphors, such as progress, individualism, economism, and evolution. The example in Chapter 2 of how

the root metaphor of mechanism is supported by a vocabulary that limits awareness of the non-mechanistic aspects of life can be used as a model. Also have them identify the vocabularies that are excluded, such as how the root metaphor of progress excludes or represents words such as tradition as sources of backwardness.

Cultural Differences between Oral and Print-based Storage and Thinking

There are many reasons that the next and perhaps last generation of scientists, technologists, engineers and mathematicians need to understand the deep and generally overlooked differences between face-to-face (oral) communication and communication through the printed word and other abstract symbols systems. Most current scientists, like others in modern culture, have been educated to take for granted a misconception perpetuated in the West, and now being imposed on the rest of the world. The misconception is that literate, print-based cultures are more enlightened, progressive, modern, and civilized than predominately oral cultures. The misconception is basic to how the word "illiterate" has been used as a pejorative term. As the digital revolution relies predominately on print and other abstract systems of representation (even the visual/voice representations are highly abstracted from the emergent living contexts), their widespread use further promotes literacy (increasingly in one of the major languages) while at the same time undermining face-to-face intergenerational communication and mentoring.

There are a number of issues related to the differences between oral and print-based cultural storage and thinking that scientists, technologists, and other experts will face as they increasingly confront questions about cultural changes that contribute to a more sustainable future. Understanding these differences requires understanding that print is a technology. And a more complex understanding of technology requires reading Jacques Ellul's *The Technological Society* (1964), as well as other books that focus on the cultural transformative nature of technologies—including how each technology needs to be understood in terms of its cultural amplification and reduction characteristics. This is not likely to happen as the ecological crisis deepens and attention shifts more to finding short and long term ways of mitigating its impact on people's daily lives. To understand the profound differences between predominately oral and print-based cultures requires reading the extensive writings of Walter Ong, Eric Havelock, and Jack Goody. Unfortunately, this in not likely to happen as the digital technologies have shortened people's attention spans and as the world shifts to a more crisis mode of consciousness, and to confronting terrorism.

Here I shall draw on both sets of authors in order to focus on several basic issues to which STEM students should be introduced—at least at the level where they can avoid the misconceptions so prominent among scientists and technologists whose scientism influences the larger public into embracing technologies and allocating resources that undermine social justice traditions and intergenerational knowledge and skills essential to avoiding the surveillance/police state mentality that is becoming more widespread.

There are two main issues that should be discussed by STEM students. The first is that if the language of one's cultural group is largely learned at the taken for granted level necessary for communicating about a reality that others also take for granted, such as thinking of time as linear, that this is a world of things (and not one of relationships), and that statements can accurately represent some aspect of the world as objective information, facts, and data, then what is spoken or represented in print has been influenced by the earlier forms of intelligence that frames the current use of words. In short, the use of language encodes earlier cultural assumptions that influenced the choice of analogs that continue to frame the meaning of word. Every statement that purports to represent what is factual and objective is in part a cultural construct—which may vary in terms of how accurately the statements take account of what has been observed. To make this point in another way, language cannot accurately provide a culturally free account of the world. There is always the presence of earlier culturally specific patterns of thinking that are part of the ecology of language. And there is the universal problem of not knowing what we do not know.

While the spoken word provides the possibility, given certain variables, of negotiating between different perspectives and uses of a shared metaphorical language, print-based cultural storage and thinking introduces a radically different set of variables—both in terms of the writer and the reader. In bringing to the attention of students the amplification and reduction characteristics of print (which is a technology), it is important to emphasize the need to keep in mind the many important uses of print. The discussion should not lead students to jump to the conclusion that it is being suggested that we should do away with print. Rather, the point that needs to be stressed is the importance of understanding the limitations inherent in print-based cultural storage and thinking.

Hopefully, this will lead to a more critical awareness of when print-based representations may lead to decisions that are destructive. For example, one of the cultural amplification characteristics of print is that it fosters abstract thinking and thus the need to ignore what can be learned from careful on-the-ground observation. The two diplomats who drew the political boundaries for the modern state of Iraq after the collapse of the Ottoman Empire following the end of World War I were highly educated in a print-based curriculum, and having been educated to think in abstractions, such as drawing the boundaries of the new state, they overlooked what even casual observation would have revealed: namely, that the tribal differences in understanding of the Muslim traditions was so great that they would be constantly in conflict with each other.

Other examples of adopting the abstract thinking of Western philosophers and social theorists that have led to today's seemingly intractable social problems can be seen in how the abstract (that is, culturally uniformed) ideas of John Locke on the origins and nature of private property, Adam Smith on the nature of free markets, René Descartes on the need to ignore traditional knowledge, and Ayn Rand's abstract explanations of the virtues of pursuing a life of selfishness, are still being carried forward as though they represent universal Truths.

After students discuss the many important, indeed indispensable uses of print, the following needs to be brought to their attention (which they can then verify in terms of their own experience):

1   What is committed to print becomes immediately dated and can only represent a surface knowledge. This same holds for what is represented as data. Neither print nor data are able to represent the emergent, relational, and interdependent cultural and natural ecological systems within which we live. To put this another way, what cultural patterns, as well as inner experiences, cannot be fully represented in print or as data? If they are taken for granted are they likely to be represented in print or as data? Can we digitize what we are not aware of? Print and data provide only surface accounts that are then subjected to being interpreted by others who are likely to be unaware of their own taken for granted cultural assumptions.

2   What is represented in print and as data has the appearance of being an objective account, but actually reflects the culturally influenced interpretative frameworks of the writer and data collector. These same taken for granted cultural patterns, including the influence of the language that encodes earlier ways of thinking, also frame how the reader and user of data will interpret the printed text or accumulated data. Even when both print and data are mediated by the use of technology, at some point a culturally influenced interpretation will enter into the process.

3   The use of print and data reinforces the cultural myth of language operating in a sender/receiver form of communication (what Michael Reddy refers to as a conduit view of language and communication). This holds that people put their supposedly original ideas and scholarly rational thoughts into words and send them to others via the use of print or as data. What is important about this sender/receiver (conduit) view of language is that it reinforces for most people the idea of objective knowledge, facts, information, and data. Print and data help to hide that words are metaphors, that they have a history, and that they continue to influence the thinking of the writer and reader in ways that she/he is too often unaware. Why is this important? Basically, the sender/receiver (conduit) view of the communication of printed accounts diverts attention from considering how the metaphorical language carries forward the ecologically problematic patterns of thinking, as well as the silences, from the past.

4   The tendency to view what appears in print and as data as objective leads to the process of reification where the supposed factual and objective nature of knowledge, facts, and so forth are assumed to be universals that all culture should live by. Third person accounts, which are reinforced in universities and the media, strengthen the tendency of readers to accept what appears in print as objective and thus as an accurate description of events, ideas, casual relationships.

Oral, that is face-to-face communication, involves all the senses, personal and communal memory, intuition, judgments about the character and veracity of the speaker, ongoing reflection on what the senses encounter in the world of ongoing changes and patterns that connect, and the possibility of negotiating between different understandings of what constitutes evidence or the meaning of what is observed.

That is, face-to-face communication, which may have many of the characteristics of print-based thinking and communication that are reinforced by years of abstract learning from books and professors who rely upon highly abstract vocabularies, possesses another characteristic largely missing in print-based thinking and communication. The asymmetrical power relationships between the printed word (including visual images) and the reader (and viewer) amplifies the many ways in which writers, media engineers, and now hackers lack a sense of moral accountability. Why exploitation in face-to-face communities is less likely to happen also applies in oral cultures where people interact face to face and are more conscious of their mutual interdependency. For example, what Gregory Stock (Ph.D. in biophysics from Johns Hopkins) wrote in his 1993 book, *Metaman: The Merging of Humans and Machines into a Global Superorganism*, would get an immediate response from the Nunavuk of the far north of Canada and from most indigenous cultures in different parts of the world if it were said face to face, rather than appearing in print far away from the people's lives. That is, he envisages their disappearance for the following reasons:

> A few centuries ago, the world brimmed with rich, distinctive cultural traditions. . . . Today such diversity is mostly a thing of the past. A few traditional cultures still persist, but their days are numbered. They cannot long withstand the seductive influences of tourists and modern communication, nor effectively isolate themselves in remote preserves. Inevitably, they too will be transformed, because mass production, instantaneous communication, specialization, and rapid change are largely incompatible with the social order of the preindustrial age.
>
> (Stock, 1993, 99)

The arguments by Francis Crick, E. O. Wilson, Richard Dawkins, and other prominent scientists that religions represented an early adaptive behavior but now have no place in a world governed by scientific inquiry, and that they should be replaced by the master narrative of science which is the story of the Earth's evolution through natural selection, would also be challenged in face-to-face conversations by followers of Mahatma Gandhi, and Martin Luther King, Jr. The glowing printed accounts of how people's lives are being improved by the digital revolution would also be challenged if made in face-to-face conversations with people who have been hacked, who have lost their skills and even their jobs to robots, and who are waking up to the deeper implications of losing their privacy and control over their own lives as their electronic footprints are transformed into data that is sold and shared among the different institutions and corporations that will use it to further their own political and economic agendas.

How STEM students respond differently to print-based accounts and to face-to-face interactions (with the latter being increasingly displaced by various digital technologies) that involve information about the world they live in needs to be discussed in the same way as the differences in other taken for granted cultural patterns. As the discussion becomes more grounded in careful reflections about the patterns of experience being made explicit, the complexity of the issues will become more apparent—as well as the reasons why scientists, when it comes to putting their thoughts into print, too often descend into the realm of scientism that does not require any accountability either for what is being misrepresented or for how technocrats and policy makers introduce changes based on their misconceptions and hubris.

Questions for Students to Consider

1   Ask students to consider what is left out of a printed account of an experience they shared together. Also, ask them to consider how the interpretative framework taken for granted by the person who writes up an account of what happened influences what is not part of the printed account. If there are students from different ethnic groups, ask how their written accounts might differ.

2   Ask students to consider how print creates a sense of authority, and thus serves a political function even when what appears in print is represented as a factual account and not as an interpretation.

3   Explore student suggestions for how to expand awareness that part of the process of reading is to be aware of the taken for granted cultural assumptions in what is written and thus the interpretative framework of the writer.

4   Discuss how the over- and un-critical reliance upon print has influenced oral communication to ignore the downside of print-based communication. Almost any recording of a politician's oral discourse, and even that of most teachers/professors as well as others who represent some area of cultural authority, can be used in assessing the extent the speaker's vocabulary reproduces the abstract world of print-based storage and thinking. The key issue

in determining when oral communication reproduces the abstract world of print is whether it fails to move to the level of dialog with others, and also fails to take into account the emergent, relational, and interdependent world shared by the speakers. If spoken words are used to represent a world of fixed entities and relationships, it is then the expression of a print-based mode of consciousness.

Questioning the Anti-tradition Traditions of Western Science

Most students will come to their first STEM courses already indoctrinated into equating innovations, new ideas, and critical inquiry with progress. And they already will have encountered many references to traditions as sources of backwardness, with the emphasis now being on how computer literacy separates the modern and progressive cultures from those still mired in backwardness. Literacy was the former basis for identifying the dividing line between the modern and pre-modern. When students read Sagan on the role of science in questioning established beliefs, computer scientists such as Hans Moravec and Ray Kurzweil on how computers will shortly (if they have not already) surpassed human intelligence, and neuroscientists working on how to make the brain more efficient and intelligent (which suggests that its current condition is a source of backwardness), students will be encountering how today's cultural elites continue to support the ecologically uniformed and ethnocentric Enlightenment thinkers of the 17th and 18th century who argued that rational thinking, science, and individual freedom should replace knowledge based on traditions.

When it comes to choosing between many of the traditions of the feudal era and the early gains in the science, in laying the basis for individual participation in the political process, and for opening the door to social mobility, the ideas of the Enlightenment represented a genuine step forward. The problem then, which has continued into the present, with many branches of science—including computer science—being complicit, is that the metaphor of tradition was framed by privileged theorists who relied upon others to provide their food, to engage in a wide variety of crafts, to build their cities, and to carry forward the traditions of knowledge later generations would expand upon. Today's scientists and technologists are carrying forward the ways in which Enlightenment thinkers narrowly framed the meaning of traditions so that only the "anti-traditions traditions" would be associated with progress. What cannot be observed, measured, and examined on an experimental basis—which includes the complex symbolic worlds of different cultures—is simply written off as superstitions. Or as Crick and Wilson claim, the symbolic dimensions of consciousness—the sources of the arts, spirituality, and aesthetic and moral values—represent what scientific advances will bring under their control (Wilson, 1998, 255).

The following statement serves as evidence of why future scientists must understand the limits of scientific knowledge, and be open to recognizing the nature and importance of traditions—especially traditions that strengthen the self reliance of communities that have a smaller ecological footprint. While Wilson does not speak for other scientists, he is widely regarded as among today's most important scientific thinkers who is also concerned about the ecological crisis. Science, as explained by Wilson, "*is the organized, systematic enterprise that gathers knowledge about the world and condenses the knowledge into testable laws and principle*" (italics in the original, 1998, 53). He further notes that scientists

> know the first rule of the professional game book: Make an important discovery, and you are a successful scientist in the true, elitist sense in a profession where elitism is practiced without shame. . . . Fail to discover, and you are little or nothing in the culture of science, no matter how much you learn and write about science.
>
> (Wilson, 1998, 56)

Wilson represents the dominant tradition within the cultures of science and technology—which is driven by the quest for the new and innovating. These values also are what have driven the industrial revolution and now the digital revolution.

The title of Eric Schmidt's and Jared Cohen's book, *The New Digital Age: Reshaping the Future of People, Nations, and Business* (2013) suggests the hubris shared within the field of computer science, as well as its indifference to the importance of the traditions being overturned in the computer scientists' rush to innovate and to create new markets. It would not be unfair to claim that the progressive, individually-centered, computer-dependent ideology that dominates the thinking within the field of computer science, which now is being adopted on a global basis, has made a virtue of nihilism that is now justified on the basis of the convenience, efficiency, and profits. Books promoting the future of the digital world that is seen as being global in nature do not mention cultural traditions, except to claim that there may be "holdouts" (such as the Amish) against the computer driven and controlled future. Diamandis and Kolter end their book by noting that "the majority of us are here for the ride. And, as should be clear by now, it's going to be quite a ride" (2012, 304).

Yes, most of us would agree that it's going to be quite a ride living in a world where privacy is only a memory, where personal security is now at the whim of hackers, where the increasingly computer addicted youth focus only on the present and their subjective explorations of cyberspace—and thus are ignorant of their culture's history, and where personal data profiles are being sold to businesses and governments that view data as the primary technology for tracking and controlling the behavior of people. It's also going to be quite a ride as natural systems undergo changes leading to extreme droughts and weather patterns, to oceans that are becoming too acidic to support fisheries already undergoing drastic declines, and as a population moving toward 9 billion continues to be caught in being increasingly dependent upon a money economy while the digital revolution, driven by the ethos of global capitalism, reduces the need for workers.

The social justice gains in the past are also examples of traditions—such as habeus corpus, gains in civil liberties and the workplace, and advances of minorities in gaining access to education, the right to vote, and to be free of police harassment. Unfortunately, these gains are being eroded as digital technologies are both changing consciousness itself where long term memory is being lost and as surveillance technnologies are strengthening the policing of people's behaviors by corporations and governments.

Questions for Students to Consider

1   As there is a connection between what we are able to name and explicit awareness (with the names often being metaphors that highlight the thinking of earlier generations as well as their silences), ask the students to identify the words beginning with the word "enlightened" that equate change with progress. Also, identify the words that equate traditions with backwardness. And have a person who speaks a non-Western language and is from an oral culture explain how traditions are viewed in her/his own culture.

2   As most traditions are re-enacted as part of a person's taken for granted knowledge and skills, ask the students to engage in an ethnographic account of the traditions they re-enact on a daily basis. It might be an ethnography of writing a paper, reading a book or on a computer screen, preparing a meal, patterns re-enacted in face-to-face communication.

3   Have students discuss their views on the connections between traditions that represent gains in civil liberties, as well as the ways these traditions are being undermined by capitalism's emphasis on profits and innovations as well as by the introduction of digital technologies.

4   A question that will push the students' thinking is how the increasing emphasis on print and data-based knowledge (which foster abstract thinking) undermines awareness of the cultural traditions that have influenced human relationships—including relationships with natural systems. In short, what are the traditions that influence how people respond to the emergent, relational, and co-dependent world of everyday experience? An example that will provide a context for recognizing the importance of this question is how the emphasis on genetic engineering of plants that will survive the use of pesticides such as Roundup, as well as increase yields that are uniform in size that enable the use of technology, leads to ignoring the ecologically informed traditions previously relied upon by farmers. What traditional forms of knowledge are relied upon when the farmers save seeds from the previous crop—rather than relying upon seeds bought from Monsanto?

5   In the higher grades, assign books written by highly recognized scientists, including a computer scientist, and have the student report on how traditions are explained. It is especially important to note whether the scientists recognize that all the advances in science are based upon the efforts of previous generations of scientists—that is, their traditions. Also, have the student give special attention to whether the scientists or computer scientists discuss the need to recognize the danger of overturning traditions, as once lost they cannot be recovered. This last point is so important, now as we see our traditions of privacy, craft knowledge, and personal security being lost as the digital revolution spreads, that it deserves discussion on the part of students. Also, does the overturning of traditions by scientists and technologists need to become the focus of community decision making? Is community resistance to fracking an example of communities awakening to the need to challenge expert knowledge?

Why Scientists and Technologists Need to be Aware of the Cultural Commons

At some point in their early STEM courses, most students will either read or have heard references to Garrett Hardin's "The Tragedy of the Commons." What their teachers/professors are not likely to mention are the commons that enable people to live less consumer dependent lifestyles—and thus less environmentally destructive lives. Part of the reason for this collective silence is the silence on the part of their professors, which has its roots in the Enlightenment ideology that most take for granted. The silence on what is perhaps the one viable alternative to the individualistic, consumer-dependent lifestyle that is being globalized can also be attributed to how participating in the cultural commons of one's family and culture is part of the daily taken for granted experiences—like writing from left to right in English, and thinking and speaking in the subject, verb, object pattern that are the tacit expectation of others in the English language community.

The taken for granted nature of the cultural commons, which vary from culture to culture and whose revitalization avoids the cultural colonization that accompanies the West's technologies, raises special problems for scientists, and especially computer scientists who want to reduce the knowable world to what can be measured and digitized as objective data. That is, the emphasis on what is observable and measurable does not take account of the larger fund of intergenerational knowledge and skills that are tacitly passed forward through face-to-face and mentoring relationships. This part of the commons represents the cultural heritage that is a mix of knowledge and skills refined over countless generations of living deeply in one place. Depending upon the cultural commons of the group, it will contain knowledge and skills about how to grow and prepare food that is healthy, how to use technologies that have been adapted to the cycles of renewal of natural systems. It may also involve passing forward biases and superstitions; both of which lead scientists to ignore learning about the aspects of intergenerational knowledge that strengthens the sense of community and the ability to live less money dependent lives—which will be needed in the future as computer systems displace the need for workers.

If scientists, computer scientists, and engineers were to adopt an ethnographic approach to learning about the cultural commons of different groups, including those in urban areas, the following would be important to focus on: the intergenerational knowledge and skills encoded in the growing, preparation, and sharing of food; knowledge of the medicinal characteristics of local plants and healing practices; ceremonies and narratives that encode the culture's moral codes; the creative arts ranging from dance, music, poetry, theatre; craft knowledge and skills in the use of a variety of materials; games; language; systems for settling disputes and providing basic protections—including what we call civil liberties; knowledge of local ecosystems and how to adapt technologies to ways that avoid damaging natural systems. Each of these aspects of the cultural commons has many sub-fields such as in the musical traditions that are part of the cultural commons.

The cultural commons are now being undermined as the world becomes more dependent upon digital technologies, and less dependent upon the intergenerational knowledge and skill passed forward through face-to-face communication. As the knowledge and skills of how to live more community-centered lives disappear when encoded as data and in printed accounts, increasing numbers of young people will face the double bind of needing employment, which will become even more limited as the digital revolution leads to computer-driven production and distribution processes that are global, while at the same time having been indoctrinated to view traditional knowledge as a source of backwardness. For them, learning to use the modern version of the Russian Kalashinkov, as well as the dream of returning to a pre-modern past, will be their way of taking revenge on a system that denies any hope other than that of becoming a martyr for a supposedly higher cause. The spread of a money economy that is unaccompanied by the availability of meaningful work, as well as access to the abstract world of the Internet with its images of endless consumerism, further undermine what is left of the local cultural commons in many parts of the world.

The Enlightenment thinking that underlies the ideology encoded in the scientific method, and was ignored in the education of earlier generations of scientists, technologists, and engineers, needs to be avoided in STEM courses. This will require introducing students to the cultural commons in the following way. First, students need to review how the metaphorical nature of language, including the role of root metaphors, carries forward earlier ways of thinking that were unaware of environmental limits and other cultural ways of knowing that achieved a high level of ecological intelligence. Second, students need an explicit knowledge of the pervasiveness of their own as well as other people's taken for granted knowledge and values—including an understanding of the nature of traditions as being sources of empowerment as well as destructive. Print-based accounts of traditions are too often sources of prejudice and too often fail to highlight the taken for granted traditions that, when made explicit, students can identify with.

After these reviews have been carried out it is then possible to have the students undertake ethnographies of the cultural commons of their own families, community, as well as the cultural commons of other cultures. The key questions to be explored relate to whether the traditions of intergenerational knowledge contribute to a morally coherent and mutually supportive lifestyle that enables people to live less consumerist and thus less environmentally destructive lives.

These concerns can be used to identify the observable evidence of the differences between cultural commons activities and those that are based on consumerism and individually-centered lifestyles. That is, do mentoring relationships in any of the cultural commons lead to discovering talents and developing skills? What are the differences between the talents and skill developed in consumer dependent relationships? Which requires greater dependency upon a money economy, and which is more likely to provide mutual support in meeting basic human needs as the ecological crisis deepens to the point where resources taken for granted in the past become increasingly limited?

There are also questions about health issues that accompany the differences between cultural commons lifestyles and the industrial/consumer dependent lifestyles where there are toxins and growing uncertainties about whether employment will be possible in the future. The issue that is the main focus of Robert Putnam's *Our Kids: The American Dream in Crisis* (2014) is that the growing inequality of wealth and opportunity to acquire the cultural capital that enabled youth of previous generations to join the middle class ceases to be an issue when the definition of wealth is reframed so that it encompasses the talents and skill that can be given back to the community. Indeed, the idea of social classes is largely the creation of a market economy where status reflects the level of material wealth. The sustainable forms of wealth within the cultural commons represent a radical shift that is more in line with the scale of Gross National Happiness developed by Bhutan as an alternative to the West's focus on gross domestic product.

It is important to engage STEM students in a discussion of whether the scientific paradigm, as well as the ideologies such as libertarianism and the Enlightenment myth of technologically driven progress, are able to account fully for the range of personal experiences that accompany involvement in cultural commons activities and relationships. Participating in mutually supportive activities, being mentored in a craft or one of the creative arts, giving back to the community, and contributing to the future that encompasses the prospects of something larger than one's self—including the non-human world, influences one's self identity, and contributes to the sense of belonging and self-worth that are denied in many social settings where money and status are keys to self-respect. The inner world of the individual, depending upon social influences, is largely beyond what can be accurately observed and measured. It is certainly beyond what can be reduced to objective knowledge as the taken for granted linguistic influences that frame what is taken to be objective knowledge can never be fully eliminated. Discussing this aspect of the students' own experience, as well as that of others, will help them recognize that the inner-subjective world of experience is beyond what can be accounted for by an MRI scan, and by efforts to explain how thousands of genes "produce the holistic properties of mind and culture" as Wilson put it (1998, 137).

Wendell Berry got it right when he criticizes the proclivity of scientism to engage in the reductionism of lived experience to what is measurable and then to the interplay of neurons and genes that are prescribed by natural forces. So much of the emergent, relational, and co-dependent processes that vary between the world cultural and natural ecologies are ignored by the epistemology of Western science and the reductionist technologies it relies upon that few scientists, technologists, and engineers are aware of when they have crossed-over into becoming agents of Western colonization. One of the dividing lines can be more easily identified if STEM students can recognize the experiential dimensions of cultural commons relationships and activities for which the scientific method cannot account.

Engaging in ethnographies of cultural commons activities that occur in a variety of social settings, including within ethnic cultures, will help bring into focus another weakness of Western science still rooted in the limited understanding of Enlightenment thinkers. And this is a weakness that STEM students must experience for themselves.

Namely, they need to be aware of the community-centered traditions that have a smaller impact on the viability of natural systems. Environmental scientists are keenly aware of the need to conserve species and habitats and thus are more aware of the cultural traditions that contribute to ecologically sustainable practices. But what are the cultural traditions that neuroscientists, computer scientists, theoretical physicists, and so forth, are willing to speak in defense of? The myth of progress, the quest for new ideas and innovations, and the reward system that supports this mythic thinking, too often results in scientists supporting the economic forces that have now put at risk the future of all cultural and natural ecologies. The current efforts to genetically modify not only seeds but also animals in ways that improve the profitability and efficiency of production systems are constant reminders, as well as the role of scientists in creating new weapon systems (with robot warriors being the latest economic growth opportunity) being a sign of the moral poverty within the diverse ranks of scientists, technologists, and engineers. With ecologically oriented scientists presenting evidence that global changes in the Earth's natural systems signal that we are well into the world's sixth extinction cycle, the billions spent on space exploration, partly justified on the grounds of finding an alternative planet to inhabit and to learn if there is another form of intelligence in the universe, are further evidence that many scientists embody too many weaknesses of character and intellect to play the Promethean role they have claimed for themselves.

Questions for Students to Consider

1   Ask students to identify how different technologies have undermined cultural commons skills and practices. The discussion should include what was gained and what was lost as a result of an innovation, with the focus being on whether the innovations contributed to an ecologically sustainable future.
2   Discuss whether an awareness of the social justice traditions as well as those related to civil liberties, such as privacy and personal security, undermines or broadens the mandate of the scientific method.
3   A question that needs discussing is whether new scientific advances, including the resulting technologies, should be subject to the democratic process. The focus might be on introducing robots into the work place, engineering genetic material in ways that affect future generations of plants, animals, and even people, and moving from face-to-face education to computer-mediated learning. The students should be reminded about the key understandings of modern science that large segments of the public now reject. Have the sciences and technologies now moved beyond the possibilities of an informed democratic process?
4   Ethno-scientific understandings and uses of technologies have always been integral to the world's diversity of cultural commons. How do these approaches to acquiring new knowledge differ from modern approaches that are accompanied by huge risks that extend beyond solving a particular problem? Does the emphasis on profits and progress set the modern approaches off from those carried forward as part of the wealth of the cultural commons?

Replacing the Myth of Individual Intelligence by Expanding the Exercise of Ecological Intelligence

There are many cultural forces that have contributed to the idea of individual intelligence. As the feudal understanding of the individual as a subject yielded over time to the idea that individuals have the potential to be autonomous thinkers and to be participants in the political process, with the former being argued by important Western philosophers including John Locke, Immanuel Kant, and Jean-Jacques Rousseau, there was little understanding of what we now recognize as the ecology of natural and cultural systems. Science was focused on the nature of things, how to group them into categories, and the importance of studying how things, material bodies, events, ideas, interacted with other autonomous entities. Mechanism was a dominant root metaphor that shaped scientific thinking, and led to an emphasis on careful observation and measurement—but also to ignoring local contexts and the surrounding cultural influences. The root metaphor of mechanism was supported by the other emerging root metaphors of the Enlightenment era, which included rational thought, individualism, and progress. That natural systems, and later cultural systems, needed to be understood as continually emergent and dependent upon their ever-changing relationships and interdependencies with other participants in the complex communication networks we now call ecologies, did not occur in the West until well into the last century. As pointed out earlier, the cultural assumptions taken for granted by the 17th- and early 18th-century thinkers continue today—including the lack of awareness of how print-based cultural storage and thinking reinforces the misconceptions of the Enlightenment thinkers—which included privileging abstract ideas over awareness of local cultural patterns.

To reiterate the main reasons that the idea of individual intelligence, as well as thinking of other aspects of life such as trees, animals, continents, rivers, and so forth as independent entities, needs to be replaced with an ecological understanding, is that everything has a history, undergoes changes resulting from the interdependencies within its environment, and should be understood as a participant within the complex information exchanges we call ecologies. As we are often able to recognize our own taken for granted patterns when pointed out by a person from another culture, it is important to take seriously how Thich Nhat Hanh, a Buddhist scholar, explains the emergent and relational nature of all life. In not being limited by the cultural assumptions encoded in the West's scientific method he is able to provide an account of life forming processes that expands the scope of the scientific gaze. He also promotes setting aside the old notions that limit awareness and thus is in agreement with Sagan's argument that awareness should not be limited by holding onto the misconceptions from the past.

But the primary misconception that must be overcome is a central feature of the reality as understood by the print-dependent philosophers and social theorists whose legacy is still taken for granted by most scientists and the general public. Namely, that things of all sorts have permanent characteristics—that is, that their characteristics and properties can be named in print, and by the use of nouns. Thich Nhat Hanh suggests that our view of reality radically changes when we give up the idea of permanence that underlies the idea of things as autonomous entities. Instead of holding onto the misconceptions handed down from the past we need to recognize the impermanence of all things.

As he put it: "Impermanence means that everything changes and that nothing remains the same in any consecutive moments. And although things change every moment, they still cannot be accurately described as the same or as different from what they were a moment ago" (2002, 40). This observation, which we all have to admit as being more accurate describes the emergent, relational, and co-dependent world we live in rather than the fictional world represented in print-based cultural storage and thinking—and now in data, leads to what he calls the world of inter-being—which is similar to what can be understood as the interactive nature of living ecological systems.

> Nothing can exist by itself alone. It has to depend on every other thing. This is called inter-being. To be means to inter-be. The paper inter-is with the sunshine and with the forest. The flower cannot exist by itself alone, it has to be inter-be with soil, rain weeds, and insects. There is no being; there is only inter-being.
>
> Looking deeply into a flower, we see that the flower is made of non-flower elements. We can describe the flower as full of everything. There is nothing that is not present in the flower. We see sunshine, we see rain, we see clouds. We see earth, and we also see time and space in the flower. A flower, like everything else, is made entirely of non-flower elements. The whole cosmos has come together in order to help the flower manifest itself. The flower is full of everything except one thing; a separate self, a separate identity.
>
> (2002, 47–48)

There is another change that comes about when the shift in awareness changes from a world of permanent things to that of inter-being; and this change is especially important to exercising a life-sustaining form of ecological intelligence. When the world of things, events, ideas, relationships are represented as autonomous, it is difficult to be aware that they are actually part of a dynamic interactive context, and that the past continues to influence the emergent nature of the present. That is, just as one's parents continue to influence today's experience, their parents, in turn were influenced by even earlier generations of parents. Just as the continuities between the past, present, and future continue in the cultural/linguistic world, as discussed in earlier chapters, they also continue in the biological world. The beetles currently destroying the forests across North America carry forward a history of evolutionary development where their destructive behavior was held in check by extreme cold temperatures, but with global warming their evolutionary potential is no longer held in check. Inter-being changes in other parts of the patterns that connect (which have a history) lead to further changes in our impermanent world.

As pointed out earlier, the dominant misconception today in the West is that there is such a thing as individual intelligence. This view is held in spite of the inter-being of having acquired a metaphorical vocabulary and interpretative frameworks that can be traced back centuries. That so many misconceptions are culturally shared—such as the idea of the inferiority of women, that we have original ideas that can be owned and monetized like real property, and so forth—should have awakened people to the mythic and destructive nature of the idea of individual intelligence. Recognizing that in spite of the traditions that continue to be a taken for granted part of everyday experience, that we each give a degree of individualized expression to a shared symbolic and environmental past should be enough for people to move on to the dominant question we all face about how to live in ecologically sustainable ways.

As I have explained elsewhere (2012, 2013, 2014, 2015), we all exercise a limited form of ecological intelligence that takes account of the impermanence of the everyday world around us, such as waiting for a red light to change, the erratic driver to pass us, the cliché-ridden conversation to end, and so forth. The taken for granted patterns of thinking are integral to this level of ecological intelligence, which means the misconceptions they carry forward from the past often impede recognizing the past influences on the present behaviors of the others, and the implications for the future that signal a further decline in our ecological prospects for the future.

The most direct way of helping STEM students recognize when they are relying upon an ecologically sustainable form of ecological intelligence is to have them examine how their taken for granted patterns of thinking, as well as those shared by others, impede awareness that permanence in whatever area of life is a myth. Almost any idea, event, behavior, organism can be used to focus a discussion on the information exchanges (the world of inter-being) that influenced what is now taken to be real and possessing a permanent condition.

In short, the exercise of ecological intelligence will be strengthened as students practice looking at their world in terms of the inter-being influences on whatever is considered to be a thing of permanence. In the language of Gregory Bateson, being aware of the inter-being influences is the same as being aware of the differences which make a difference—that is, the information exchanges and pathways between the different participants in the local ecology that interacts within the larger ecological systems. What are the foods that sustain health, and the comments that alter the individual's self-esteem, and what are the patterns of interaction with others that lead to the discovery of a personal talent—and how do the emergent qualities manifested by the changes in the individual's thought and behaviors contribute to the emergent qualities in others?

One of the primary goals of promoting a deeper level of ecological intelligence is to enable students to recognize the relational world they live in, which may take many forms—including recognizing the relationships between consumerism, individualism, and the further destruction of natural systems that others rely upon. It is learning to recognize the relationships between advertising, and the shaping of people's taken for granted level of consciousness. It also involves recognizing the inter-being world of people's behaviors and values that are not centered upon consumerism, but rather on the sharing of skills, talents, and mutual support systems that have a smaller ecological footprint.

The non-subjectively-centered exercise of ecological intelligence also leads to being aware of the lived traditions (which are profoundly different from the abstract ideas of traditions learned from print-based theorists) that need to be carried forward—and will undergo changes as they are intergenerationally renewed. These traditions are re-enacted and transformed into living processes when people come together to exchange goods and services such as on market days, rather than the abstract idea of free markets that do not take account of local cultural traditions. These are the traditions that undergo new forms of manifestation as they undergo re-interpretation by succeeding generations who are, in turn, influenced by the impermanence in their world.

Viewing the inter-being forces that are the basis of the impermanent world we live in also leads to recognizing that the ability to give attention to, and to interpret, the influences of past and current relationships will vary between cultures. There is, in effect, no one form of ecological intelligence as the languaging, taken for granted patterns of thinking, and interactions with others (who are also part of the world of impermanence) vary with contexts—including the natural environment that is also part of the ecology of impermanence. But the recognition of impermanence does not mean that nothing matters. The external forces that are manifested in the flower can also become the forces that limit the full expression of the flower—and to even limit it coming into being. The external forces that nurture self-confidence and the wisdom of being able to give back to the community may be replaced by external forces that become manifested in violent and environmentally destructive behavior.

In developing a clearer awareness of the emergent nature of relationships, and the larger cultural and natural ecology of which they are an integral part, the important questions that now need to become second nature are to ask what traditions are being carried forward that were not based on an awareness of ecological limits, but instead on the misconceptions of abstract thinkers ranging from philosophers, social theorists, theologians, and scientists whose hubris has led them to become proponents of scientism. When STEM students acquire this habit of asking about the colonizing nature of technological innovations, and whether the beliefs and practices contribute to living in interdependent communities that have a smaller toxic and carbon footprint, then their education will have overcome many of the limitations that characterize the education of past generations of scientists and technologists. As demonstrated in the inter-being forces that lead to the manifestation of the flower, such as sunshine, water, quality soils, good seeds, and so forth, the forces of inter-being that affect the lives of people not only include the physical environment but also the traditions we call culture. And it is the latter that has been largely overlooked in the education of previous generations of scientists and technologies—which is reflected in their silence about the cultural traditions that need to be conserved and those that need to be radically changed.

Questions for Students to Consider

1   How does Thich Nhat Hanh's statement "the flower is full of everything except one thing: a separate self, a separate identity" lead to rethinking other supposed separate identities such as the individual, a market, an idea, and

so forth? Is there part of your identity that has not been influenced by the processes of inter-being?

2   How does the printed word reinforce the idea of separate and fixed identities? Does data overcome this problem? What are the implications of impermanence for how we think about objective knowledge? Does awareness of impermanence depend upon an awareness that the past continues to influence the present, and that everything is in constant communication with everything else? Are these essential characteristics of exercising ecological intelligence?

3   How does computer-mediated thinking and communication reinforce the myth of individual intelligence, as well as a world of things that can be understood independent of their contexts?

4   Do the various expressions of scientism—such as expressed in the claim that computer intelligence is exceeding human intelligence, that genetic engineering is on the verge of creating a separate GeneRich species of humans, and that the epic narrative of evolution should now replace the world's religions—require a reductionist way of thinking where the world can be reduced to a few variables that can be controlled by scientists and technologists?

Re-thinking the Historical and Ideological Relationships between Science, Technology, and Capitalism

The Janus nature of science and technology needs to be understood as leading to the knowledge and technologies that have vastly improved the quality of daily life, but also as having played a key role in the development of the industrial revolution that was guided by cultural assumptions that did not take account of environmental limits and that promoted the exploitation of workers and now consumers as necessary to achieving greater profits and control of markets. As pointed out in earlier sections, it is important for STEM students to understand the language issues that frame how problems are understood as well as how the taken for granted interpretative frameworks framed by the language advantages certain groups over others—as well as impacts the prospects of an ecologically sustainable future. The previously discussed areas—the nature and importance of the cultural commons, the need to be aware of traditions that are being lost because of the progressive ideology that drives technological innovations, the need to discuss the complicity of scientists and technologists in promoting global capitalism—are cultural issues that also need to be part of the discussion of how hybrid capitalism, which is focused on community values and reducing the economic impact on natural systems, differs from corporate capitalism which is guided by abstract ideas such as free and global market systems, and the equally abstract ideas about data and profits.

The anti-tradition traditions include both science and capitalism, as well as the widely held assumption that the primary purpose of critical inquiry is to overturn all forms of traditional knowledge. Unfortunately, this anti-tradition mindset has led to ignoring the importance of historical knowledge. The digital revolution is now strengthening this anti-tradition tradition by virtue of what it is unable to represent other than as an abstraction. One of the problems is that the loss of a historical perspective, in addition to leaving people less aware of what community enhancing traditions are being overturned by the relentless expansion of the market economy, has included the loss of awareness of the historical roots of the dominant ideologies that guided development in the West. This, in turn, has led to the Orwellian transformation in our political language where the traditional meanings of our political language have been reversed to the point where dominant economic and technological forces that are transforming daily life in ecologically unsustainable ways are being labeled as conservative. And with "conservative" and "conservatism" being considered a pejorative political category by people concerned with environmental and social justice issues, they are left with the vocabulary of liberalism—which has its roots in the abstract theories of John Locke, Adam Smith, René Descartes, Immanuel Kant, and other Enlightenment theorists who were unaware of environmental limits and their own ethnocentrism.

The current misuse of the words conservative and conservatism, which market liberals and libertarians in the Ayn Rand mold took over in the 1980s and has now merged with the Tea Party Movement, has led to the mis-education of the current generation of political commentators whose voices and misconceptions now dominate the media. One of the results is that most people dependent upon the fragments of information acquired between television commercials and from other media in search of the latest disaster that will improve the size of their audience is that the larger public is unaware of the history of the different strands of reflective conservatism that warned against, among other issues, the tyranny of abstract ideas, the loss of craft knowledge and skill, and the exploitive nature of the capitalism and the Industrial Revolution that was destroying communities.

Few of today's generation of supposedly educated people are likely to have read the early critics of the Industrial Revolution that were misnamed, as Charlene Spretnak points out, as the "romantic poets" (2011). Nor are they likely to have read Edmund Burke, T.S. Eliot, Michael Oakeshott, and Mahatma Gandhi, or today's environmental conservatives such as Aldo Leopold, Wendell Berry, Helena Norberg-Hodge, and Vandana Shiva. It would not be too far off the mark to claim that the ideological sophistication of most Americans, including university graduates, is limited to a few key ideas of the classical liberal philosophers such as John Locke, Adam Smith, and Herbert Spencer that have been turned into context-free clichés that lend themselves to being integrated into various fundamentalist religious doctrines. Nor would it be off the mark to claim that these libertarian, market liberal, Tea Party faux conservatives are unaware that as the ecological crisis deepens to the point where water, protein, and digital technologies reduce the possibility of earning a living in the money-dependent economy, their survival will depend upon the traditions of the cultural commons that are being destroyed by the free market and technological policies they support.

Given the increasing rate of global warming, it is especially important that students taking STEM classes become aware of the more ecologically and culturally grounded forms of conservatism they should support, and how these forms of conservatism differ from the abstract ideas that have been carried forward by the followers of the Enlightenment philosophers who combined ignorance of environmental limits with a taken for granted attitude toward their right to be served by exploiting the labor of the under classes of their day. Students in STEM classes need to be aware not only of the history of reflective conservatism that challenged the exploitive nature of the market liberalism that provided the conceptual direction and moral legitimacy to the industrial and now digital revolution, but also of the history of conservative thinking among scientists and environmental activists that can be traced back in America to the early years of the 20th century.

Aldo Leopold's environmental classic, *A Sand County Almanac* (1949) provided the conceptual and moral cornerstone of environmental conservatism that most environmental scientists now take for granted when he wrote, "A thing is right when it tends to preserve the integrity, stability, and beauty of the biotic community. It is wrong when it tends otherwise" (262). However, the focus on conserving natural resources goes back much further in American history; but it was too often understood in terms of progressive market values. For example, as Donald Worster reports, Gifford Pinchot was the force behind the organization of the U.S. Forest Service and the chief spokesperson for the "progressive conservative" ideology that had as one of its goals the elimination of predators regarded then as limiting the productivity of the land (1977, 266). John Muir, the founder of the Sierra Club, and chief critic of the war on predators, helped put the country on the path to conserving vast areas of wilderness such as the national parks. More recently, the conservancy movement has taken a more populist turn with citizens placing their lands in special trusts that prevent them from being used for commercial purposes. Whether it was the ecological conservatism of Rachel Carson who warned about the disruptive impacts of technologies on natural systems, or the ecological conservatism of Kris and Douglas Tompkins who purchased hundreds of thousands of acres in Chile and Argentina in order to create national parks that will be in perpetuity free of economic exploitation, we see the genuine expressions of a conservatism that recognizes the long-term interdependence of humans and natural systems.

Today, there are more grass roots expressions of conservatism that challenge the faux conservative followers of Ayn Rand's libertarianism, the think tanks such as the CATO and the American Enterprise Institutes, the Republican/Tea Party politicians, and the corporations working to undermine the consensus among scientists that human activity (meaning mainly corporate excesses) is a major contributor to global warming and to the rapid acidification of the world's oceans. These include the Slow Food Movement, various localism movements mostly centered on strengthening traditions of mutual support and self sufficiency (best expressed in the Transition movement that is spreading globally), efforts to shift to local currencies, exchanges, and sharing. Perhaps most important of all, the conservatism of indigenous cultures reflected in their efforts intergenerationally to renew the traditions of their cultural commons. The pull on their youth by digital technologies highlights the tensions between the intergenerational ecologically-centered conservatism of most indigenous cultures and the market liberalism that emphasizes a world of continual change, monetized relationships, and individual autonomy.

Being realistic, it is unlikely that teachers of STEM classes will have the time or motivation to read the classic statements on reflective conservatism. They can, however, read environmental and community-centered conservatives such as Vandana Shiva, Helena Norborg-Hodge, and Wendell Berry. At the same time, they should engage in a personal ethnography of the many ways they re-enact the traditions of their own family and cultural group's cultural commons. Combined with the urgent questions raised by how the digital revolution is undermining traditions such as privacy, craft knowledge and work opportunities, traditions of civil liberties where guilt had to be established in a court of law, and democratic decision making, identifying what is personally important to conserve, in addition to the environmental scientists' commitment to conserving species and habitats, will make it easier to engage students in discussions about the differences between life sustaining expressions of conservatism and the faux conservatism that has taken over the media, as well as infected like a virus both state and national politics.

Introducing STEM students to an ecological interpretive framework of learning about the core issues in science, technology, engineering, and mathematics—which means learning to think relationally where identities change depending upon the emergent nature of contexts rather than thinking mechanistically—leads to understanding that everything has a history, is part of larger interdependent systems, and has future implications that do not always lead to progress. It is this understanding—this cautionary rather than progressive expectation—that also leads to raising the moral issues so absent in the thinking of scientists and technologists who are promoting various schemes for changing the world in ways dictated by their area of scientific expertise. Whether it is a question of how to genetically engineer a new animal that fits the industrial process, introduce new pesticides, promote the further extension of the Internet of Everything, and how to manipulate people's expectations in ways that will foster more consumerism, there is always the moral question of what contributes to strengthening community traditions of self-sufficiency and helps to check the growth of a consumer dependent lifestyle that is destroying the environment. Being dependent upon the emergent, relational, and interdependent world of the cultural and environmental ecologies means that there is no retreat from making decisions that involve moral decisions. The inter-being, as Thich Nhat Hanh points out, involves influencing the Other in ways that are carried forward over many generations—and which, like the ripple spreading across the water, affects changes throughout the interconnected ecologies.

Questions for Students to Consider

1   Ask students to engage in a personal ethnography of the traditions they want to conserve, and to identify why these traditions are important to living more ecologically sustainable lives. Also, have them discuss the cultural differences in how conserving is understood—as well as the conserving role of different cultural traditions such as the arts, narratives, protection of civil liberties, and so forth. It is important that the discussion of conserving and an ecologically sustainable form of conservatism be culturally grounded—and not reduced to a series of abstract principles and slogans.
2   Discuss whether achievements in social justice and environmental awareness and practices have their roots in liberal or conservative traditions and, if in the former, whether the gains then become part of the legacy that is to be conserved and intergenerationally renewed by future generations.
3   Raise the question of how different ideologies—market liberalism, libertarianism, reflective and culturally grounded conservatism, and people who mistakenly assume that traditions should not change—lead to different moral values. What are the implications of these differences for scientists and technologists?
4   Discuss how the scientific method needs to be revised in ways that enable future generations of scientists and technologists to recognize that their commitment to conserving species and habitats should also extend to conserving ecologically sustainable cultural traditions. How should the scientific method, as articulated by Carl Sagan, E. O. Wilson, Francis Crick, and Lee Silver, be revised?
5   Discuss the connections between the highly specialized knowledge of scientists and technologists (such as computer scientists) and the nature of hubris that leads them to promote cultural changes without considering the unintended destructive consequences. Is hubris a psychological force that leads to supporting a liberal ideology? Why is a reflective and ecologically grounded conservative less likely to be driven by hubris?

The Dangers of Mixing Liberal Ideologies with the Theory of Evolution

As STEM students will have encountered the evolutionary framework for understanding how change occurs in the heritable traits of biological populations over successive generations, it is important that they be engaged in a discussion of what cannot be explained without drifting into the fog of scientism that supports an ideological agenda in the same way as the theory of intelligent design supports a fundamentalist religious agenda. What separates the science of how natural selection accounts for a wide range of biological adaptations from the imperialism of scientism is the theory of memes introduced by Richard Dawkins in *The Selfish Gene* (1976). Uncritically adopted by E. O. Wilson and integrated into his theory of sociobiology, and further popularized by Richard Dennett, the idea of a cultural meme is supposed to represent different units of cultural norms, practices, and symbolic systems—and thus to function within the evolutionary process in ways that replicate the role of genes.

To understand what the theory of cultural memes shares in common with the core assumptions shared by both classical and neo-liberalism it is necessary to recall what is distinctive about liberal ideologies. Whether grounded in the taken for granted assumptions of Western philosophers or in a mix of Ayn Rand's theory for achieving a life of selfishness and abstract economic theories derived from Milton Friedman and his followers, liberalism supports the ideas of competitive individualism, a linear view of progress, and a human-centered view of the world. Liberal ideologies are also distinctive in proposing that these ideas are universals and should be promoted throughout the world. Aside from the problem of deciding how to represent the world's diversity of cultural patterns, mores, traditions, mythopoetic narratives—and especially the taken for granted cultural patterns—as memes that have the same standing as genes whose behavior can be observed, there is another major problem with the theory of memes.

That is, as we see in the writings of computer scientists who claim that the digital revolution that is undermining traditional cultures, and even displacing human intelligence, is guided by the forces of natural selection, they interpret evolution as leading to a form of progress that is linear and that is monolithic. In effect, their interpretation of how the technologies they introduce into cultures of which they have only the most surface understanding matches the chief characteristics of liberal/progressive ideologies. By claiming that their technological innovations now leading to the loss of privacy, personal security from hackers, loss of work opportunities as corporations seek more profits, and to the loss of intergenerational communication, are dictated by the same evolutionary processes that have guided the first self-replicating RNA molecules down different evolutionary pathways, the scientism of the computer scientists enables them to avoid taking moral responsibility. Their innovations are simply under the control of the forces of natural selection. As we have seen in recent history, it is easy to take the next step by claiming that a police state is based on a clearer understanding of the forces of natural selection, and that those whose behaviors and ideas are deemed as reactionary should be eliminated. The theory of memes, in effect, is so open to interpretation that there are no safeguards from it becoming a new version of social Darwinism.

The attacks on religion by E. O. Wilson, Richard Dawkins, Daniel Dennett, as well as the more rank and file scientists that treat the theory of evolution as a total explanatory framework for understanding the world's diversity of cultures and the language systems upon which they are based represents an extreme form of reductionist thinking. As Wendell Berry put it, this attempt to explain values, beliefs, meanings, wisdom, as well as the sources of evil that seem an inescapable aspect of human experience, as directed by the forces of natural selection is an extreme example of cultural imperialism that shares many of the characteristics of modern totalitarian systems.

There is no mystery to life for these scientists, and no sense of caution about engineering new forms of life, as seen in the proposal of Lee Silver to create a new strain of GeneRich humans or the scientists who are now working on how to reverse engineer the human brain in order to create self-aware robots. Their research agenda includes how to introduce chemicals that will lead to the loss of bad memories, which can then be used by corporations and governments to define good memories as those that support the corporate and governmental agendas. These totalitarian trends have already been well developed by the life-defining language of patriotism and consumerism, but the scientists want to ensure that the experimental uses of chemicals play a more predictable and measurable role.

The many ways that the scientific method reinforces the myth that scientists are free of cultural influences can be seen in the way that hundreds of thousands of chemicals have been introduced into the environment for the purpose of solving specific technical and social problem. Between 1930 and 2000 the amount of manmade chemicals introduced into the environment increased from 1 million to 400 million tons per year. Little was understood about how the PCBs and dioxins, for example, affected people's health or their impact on other living systems. Yet, the introduction of these life altering chemicals was justified on the basis of a number of taken for granted cultural assumptions—with the foremost assumption being the West's understanding of a linear form of progress. Economic values as well as the assumption about the environment being an endlessly exploitable resource were also taken for granted. Other cultural patterns of thinking taken for granted by these STEM graduates of earlier eras included a total indifference to considering the diversity of traditions that were being overturned by their efforts to contribute to economic and technological progress.

We are just beginning to obtain a fuller accounting of the damage done to human health and to the world's natural systems. The current rate at which white male babies are being born with various degrees of autism is now 1 in 68, which has increased from 1 in 88 births in 2012. Other illnesses resulting from the toxic chemicals that saturate every aspect of the environment are also increasing as a result of the taken for granted cultural assumptions that guided the research and technological innovations of earlier generations of scientists, technologists, engineers, and mathematicians. It is very likely their legacy will have the greatest impact on the lives of young students, now entering their first STEM courses, when they reach late middle age when it is predicted that the pH (acidification) of the world's oceans will have moved from its current level of 8.1 to 7.8. What may appear as a small change in the pH level will actually have a devastating impact on the oceans' ecologies and thus on the fisheries humans are dependent upon.

That there is something fundamentally wrong with the highly specialized education of scientists and technologists who have achieved such seemingly miraculous achievements in the realm of digital technologies, in curing diseases, and exploring outer space, can be seen in how little attention is being given to the mounting evidence that the environmental crisis, which is understood in terms of climate change, extreme weather leading to massive floodings and droughts, and to the inability of species to adapt to changes in habitats, is also a crisis in cultural ways of knowing—which scientists and technologists continue to promote globally. Billions are being spent on the technologies that will enable a few scientists to travel to Mars, on the quest to find other planets to which humans can escape as the Earth's natural systems fail, and to locate in space whether there are other forms of intelligent life. And how much of our resources are devoted to the re-engineering of the mind by neuroscientists whose own education left them largely unaware of the information and semiotically varied pathways that connect all forms of live within the interconnected cultural and environmental ecologies? Scientism needs to be understood as encompassing more than the examples of the computer scientists whose hubris leads them to introduce fundamental changes in cultures of which they have little understanding, the Lee Silvers of the scientific community that are re-engineering the genetic basis of life in ways that increase the efficiency and profits of the industrial system that continues to trash the environment, and those who want the world's cultures to adopt an expanded version of Darwin's theory of evolution as their moral framework. Scientism needs to be understood as a complicit part of applied science where the scientists and technologists take for granted the progressive nature of their innovations.

Just as there are degrees of hubris and cultural indifferences, there are degrees of scientism. And those who are less involved in promoting scientism are those who give careful attention to whether the cultural traditions threatened by their innovations contribute to sustainable cultural and natural ecologies.

Subjects to be Discussed by Students

As STEM students should now be aware of the different cultural issues ignored by various expressions of scientism, it would be useful to ask them to think about how scientism is central to the growing field of data science that relies upon software algorithms that derive from vast amounts of data decisions and step-by-step procedures for solving problems. In using the short discussion in the next chapter of what is lost when culturally influenced everyday experiences are reduced by the technologies of print and data, suggest that students identify what aspects of culturally mediated experience are ignored in data science decisions. Also, ask them to consider who gains and who loses politically and economically from reducing the world of experience to the supposedly objective status of data? A third level of discussion should focus on how decisions in science could be used to slow the level of environmental degradation—and whether providing people with data-based scenarios of how to reduce carbon dioxide and methane gases that are imperiling humanity's future will lead to changes in thinking and behavior. What is it that religious narratives and exemplary figures such as Mahatma Gandhi provide that may have a greater influence on changing people's behavior than relying upon data-based decisions? As data science is being increasingly considered as providing strategies and policies for addressing today's problems, and the algorithms are dependent upon mathematics, what questions should mathematicians be aware of if they are to limit data science becoming another example of scientism?

Challenging the Myth that Science is Morally Neutral

The widely held view within the Western scientific community that science is morally neutral is based on a number of cultural assumptions that are now being recognized as fundamentally wrong. The early scientists started with the premise that it is possible to set aside current ways of thinking, including superstitions that had been handed down for generations, and to observe the behavior of the natural world. That is, they were unaware, and still are largely unaware, of how the layered metaphorical roots of their own language continue to tacitly influence their way of thinking, including the ideas that they are autonomous observers (free of cultural influences), that their observations and testing of hypotheses which are then encoded in print (as though print is free of cultural assumptions), and communicated in ways that rely upon a conduit view of language to colleagues can replicate the experiment. In addition to ignoring the ecology of language that is an inescapable part of scientific inquiry, which represents the external world as constituted by discrete entities that can be broken into smaller entities that can be re-engineered in ways that provide humans with greater control and predictability, the combination of assumptions about the objectivity of the scientific gaze and systems of encoding objective knowledge as well as the taken for granted assumption that the scientific mode of inquiry is an inherently progressive force has led to the equally simplistic idea that the scientific method, and thus the scientists, is a morally free agent. This myth supports the other taken for granted myths about objective knowledge, the use of words to represent real entities and process, and being an outside observer of an external world.

What we now understand about ecologies, including both natural and cultural ecologies, is that everything communicates through different semiotic pathways, that all forms of existence are relational, and, as Thick Nhat Hanh points out, that impermanence characterizes all forms of life. This holds for the scientists, the use of language, and what is being observed and tested. What is especially important to recognize is the relational nature of the scientists, technologists, engineers, and mathematicians with the other participants in the cultural and natural ecologies they share together. As their existence is always relational there is the question of how their actions affect the other participants. The myth of progress allowed scientists to ignore their complicity for the unanticipated consequences of their discoveries, or as in the case of supporting intelligence testing, the eugenics movement, the introduction of toxic chemicals contributing to a host of illnesses, and now the cultural losses resulting from the digital revolution, to adopt the fallback position articulated by Carl Sagan that "science has built-in, error-correcting machinery at its very heart" (1997, 30).

In an era of expanding economies, when populations had not yet exploded beyond what natural systems could sustain, and when there was little visual evidence of the degradation of natural systems actually leading to the collapse of natural systems as we are now witnessing with the world fisheries and the Ogallala Aquifer, the destructive outcomes of scientific research were always weighted against the positive gains—and dismissed as momentary errors. The old illusions about progress continuing to bypass the destructive effects of science are no longer possible to maintain except for the ideologues trapped in their culture's myths. The myth of the morally free nature of scientific research and development is being further challenged by the stealth nature of the digital revolution. Collecting massive amounts of data on every aspect of daily life, as well as the ability of computer programs to make decisions previously made by humans, including in the workplace, are threatening civil liberties, basic securities, and disrupting the intergenerational sharing of skills and ideas essential to the cultural commons that have a smaller ecological impact. The new possibilities made available by recent scientific advances include the development of mini-drones under the control of terrorists that can carry out lethal attacks, the ability to use ordinary laboratory and gene-splicing equipment to revive extinct viruses and to produce deadly chemicals whose formulas are available on the Internet—as well as instructions on how to create a bomb, and the increasing use of algorithms for making decisions about peoples' economic and social well-being.

Students taking STEM courses need to recognize that the old ideology that supposedly shielded scientists, technologists, engineers, and mathematicians from recognizing that they are not free of taking moral responsibility for their discoveries and technological innovations is no longer acceptable. That is, moral issues surrounding the introduction of robots, algorithms, drones, life altering gene-splicing technologies, Big Data, and so forth need to be identified and examined in terms of how they impact different segments of society—including other cultures. For example, the myth of progress, reinterpreted by E. O. Wilson as cultural changes resulting from the forces of natural selection, which leads him to give scientific legitimation to the argument that all the world's religions should be abandoned on the grounds of representing earlier stages in cultural adaptation, contributes to secularizing moral values (which in turn promotes the Western values of individualism and materialism). Does he have a moral responsibility for contributing to undermining the meta-narratives that are the basis of the moral codes of other cultures, and for the intergenerational alienation within these cultures?

Questions for Students to Consider

1 If we live in a world that is relational, impermanent, and is an ecology of past influences and future possibilities, are there examples of scientific knowledge, technologies, and development that do not have moral implications?

2 Do scientists and others have a responsibility to consider how their discoveries will be used—including who benefits and who will be the losers?

3 What are the conceptual/moral frameworks that scientists, technologists, engineers, and mathematicians can rely upon in making their own moral decisions—or are moral decisions to be guided by the subjective judgment of the individual?

4 Should the beliefs and values of the cultures that will be affected by the new scientifically derived knowledge and technologies be taken into account—and in some instances be the basis for what constitutes a right or wrong decision? For example, should scientists and technologists work for the corporation that is introducing genetically modified seeds into a culture such as India where farmers face limited possibility of being financially viable—and where there is now a high rate of suicides?

5 How do scientists working for corporations and the Department of Defense explain their supposedly amoral stance? What are the misconceptions held by the larger society that enable scientists and their collaborators to push onto others the moral responsibility for how their discoveries and innovations are used for destructive purposes? Are they simply doing what is necessary to earn a living, and to contribute to progress, to protect America from its enemies?

6 In order to connect the discussion of moral issues to the root metaphors that guide the thinking of scientists and technologists, ask students to discuss how the different root metaphors of patriarchy, anthropocentism, individualism, progress, mechanism, economism, evolution, and ecology influence how moral values are understood. Having students identify the vocabularies that support each root metaphor, or combination of root metaphors, will help identify what will be viewed as moral and immoral within the context of each root metaphor.

6

HOW AN UNCRITICAL RELIANCE UPON PRINT AND DATA MISREPRESENTS THE EMERGENT, RELATIONAL, AND INTERDEPENDENT WORLD OF ALL ECOLOGIES

Given the deepening ecological crisis and the violence spreading around the world, it important to consider how print and data misrepresent the emergent, relational, and interdependent nature of human experience as well as how both contribute to a colonizing process that undermines the face-to-face intergenerational knowledge of the world's diverse cultural and natural ecologies. Both the uses of print and data are widely assumed to be technologies that contribute to modern development. Thus, it's important that a different conceptual framework be used to explain how it is that print and data have indeed been used in many socially constructive ways, and how an uncritical use fosters abstract thinking that, in turn, undermines the exercise of ecological intelligence that recognizes that impermanence is a basic characteristic of all forms of life.

The conceptual framework discussed in an earlier chapter will also be relied upon here as the ancient Romans' understanding of Janus as the god of new beginnings—or as I would put it, the god overseeing the emergent, relational, and co-dependent life forming and sustaining processes. Janus had two faces, which looked in opposite directions—one face oversaw the constructive nature of new beginnings, while the other face oversaw how new beginnings led to destructive ends. If we rely upon this conceptual/moral framework we can then discuss what is destructive and ecologically problematic about the uncritical uses of print and data while at the same time acknowledging that both are important and now indispensable.

The West has a long history of elites promoting the idea that the higher and more reliable form of knowledge is encoded in print, and now in data. This is the history of abstract thinkers in the West, ranging from Plato to Milton Friedman—and now includes the experts who are promoting the digital revolution that is transforming education, the work place, and everyday life into a near total surveillance culture that benefits corporations and governmental agencies with close ties to the military establishment. Printed rules served in the past to protect civil liberties from the emotional upheavals prompted by the heat of rumor, journalism, and now the Internet. But then as now printed rules were unable to provide a full and accurate account of the mix between the fixed conceptual world of taken for granted beliefs and patterns of thinking and the impermanence that characterizes living systems—including humans where emotions, meanings, identity, values, thoughts, internal biological processes and behaviors continually change in response to the changes occurring in other systems that are part of the environment. In addition to Thich Nhat Hanh's insights about impermanence and how the "inter-being" of everything from a flower to an idea such as data is at each phase of development the accumulation of past influences, there is Gregory Bateson's seemingly enigmatic statement that the "difference which makes a difference" is the basic unit of information that sets in motion a succession of responses to differences that sustain both cultural and natural ecological systems. Recognizing the central role of differences that make a difference in the information (semiotic) pathways of both environmental and cultural ecologies is another way of emphasizing that there are no fixed, unchanging things. Everything exists in relationships that undergo constant change—except for what appears in print or as data. But then it also undergoes a continual process of interpretation and then reinterpretation, given the changes in the users culturally influenced patterns of thinking.

Both print and now the increasing reliance upon data are unable to represent in real time the impermanence of living processes. As pointed out earlier, what is represented in print and as data is immediately dated and at best provides only a surface account of the differences which make a difference. The dated and surface account is lost sight of because print and data introduce a different way of representing reality. That is, they both shift the focus away from the impermanence that leads to a constant flow of information exchanges. What is represented as real is the abstract world where the printed word or what has been digitized lead to a second basic misrepresentation—namely, that what appears in print or as data can be understood as providing an objective account of a fixed reality. The European settlers displacing the indigenous cultures across the land were driven by a sense of "manifest destiny" and their drive to "truck, barter, and trade" was rooted in competitive individualism made possible by free markets. Both are abstract statements to which the technology of print and digitization give the appearance of factualness and objectivity. But where is the impermanence in the emotions, sense of empowerment, and later reflections of the writer who realizes these earlier misconceptions that others took to be a universal truth?

With print- and data-based learning in schools now being further narrowed by the increased reliance upon computers the process of socializing students into becoming abstract thinkers who rely less on what is learned through the senses and from face-to-face communication is taking an even more ecologically destructive turn. It is the personal senses, memory, intuition, and the ongoing negotiation of meanings that are part of face-to-face communication that are responsive to the impermanence of life sustaining processes as work is carried out, in carrying on a conversation, in adjusting behaviors and expectations as droughts prevent seeds from sprouting—which is just the beginning of the possible social chaos that few people are prepared to think about.

Ironically, while everyone, regardless of culture, adjusts their everyday decisions in ways that take account of the emerging, relational, and interdependencies within their field of experience, whether in conversations, in using a technology, or in preparing a meal, the mythic idea of individual intelligence has been so dominant that few Westerners have understood how their own individually centered and limited exercise of ecological intelligence in responding to the emergent and relational changes have been influenced by the print-based abstractions passed forward as part of learning to think in the language whose meanings were framed by the analogs settled upon by earlier generations. How many generations of philosophy students have studied the abstract ideas of Plato, and other mainstream Western philosophers, without realizing that their ideas were ethnocentric and near totally uninformed by the traditions that sustained the cultural commons of their eras—some of which were the beginnings of what have become part of our traditions of civil liberties.

As pointed out in earlier chapters, the following characteristics of print and data have largely been ignored. Yet ignorance of these overlooked characteristics has not diminished their increasing importance in undermining the ethnic and intergenerational differences in the exercise of ecological intelligence that depends upon an explicit awareness of the emergent and relational nature of life forming and sustaining processes within local and global ecological systems. The abstract world of print and data is very different. To reiterate what is too easily overlooked (repressed) is that what is represented in print and as data is immediately dated, and provides only a surface account of the emergent, relational, and interdependent nature of everyday life. That is, they both misrepresent the contexts of people's lives, events, and ideas in ways that ignore the history of cultural influences as well as the uniqueness of self-expression and efforts to transcend the limitations of one's inherited language.

To reiterate another key point: both print and data rely upon a conduit (that is, sender/receiver) view of language that hides that words have a history, and are metaphors that encode the analogs of earlier thinkers. This means, in effect, that words (metaphors) such as "woman," "data," "tradition," "intelligence," "individualism," may carry forward the taken for granted patterns of thinking that reproduce the misconceptions, biases and silences of the past. By ignoring that the metaphorical basis of our language includes root metaphors such as anthropocentrism, mechanism, progress, and so forth, that are the basis of our taken for granted interpretative frameworks, we are unaware of the alternative realities hidden by these root metaphors.

Other characteristics of how print and data misrepresent the world in which we live include how what is represented in print or as data reflects the taken for granted interpretative framework of the writer and data collector. The combination of the conduit view of language that hides that words are metaphorical and reproduce earlier misconceptions and silences, along with the printed word and data, lead to another basic misrepresentation. Namely, that what appears in print and as data is too often understood as being free of cultural influences and thus as objective facts, information, and data. Both the printed word and data, especially when written as third person accounts promoted in universities and the media (which are centers dedicated to abstract thinking and supposedly objective information) lend themselves to being reified and thus turned into universals that ignore differences in cultural origins and contexts. At this point the technologies of print and data take on a more colonizing role that hides behind the facade of objective and factual knowledge. The misconceptions learned in the earliest grades that ignore that words are metaphors that carry forward the specific assumptions and silences of earlier eras in a culture, make it difficult to recognize that facts and data are not objective, but represent a cultural way of knowing.

The life experiences, events, and ideas represented in print and as data, which can only be selectively represented, undergo a basic transformation (or should it be called victimization?) as a result of the writers' and data collectors' taken for granted biases, ideology, and silences acquired in their own prior socialization to how to think in the language being passed forward in their culture. In effect, what is abstracted from the ecology of relationships and personal decisions, and encoded in print or as data, represents the initial level of involuntarily surrendering one's life to being an object of interpretation by others—which may lead to a loss of a job, to being hacked, to becoming a subject of interest to the government or a corporation seeking an exploitable opportunity. What the reader and the experts now referred to as "data scientists" do with how the technology of print and data reduces the emergent ecology of life world experiences to static objective information and facts also becomes beyond the control of the individual.

To reiterate a key point made earlier, print and data are unable to give a full account of the local contexts (ecologies) of people's lives. And what is abstracted from the lived experiences within the emergent and relational cultural and natural ecologies not only encodes the taken for granted assumptions of the writer and data collector but also sets the stage for yet another assault on the truth. What appears in print and as data is then used according to the political and economic agenda of individuals and groups who feel no accountability for how they are exploiting other people's lives—such as reducing them to being consumers of products they are conditioned to want. This process of becoming an object for the Other also involves the loss of one's political voice.

Face-to-face and intergenerationally connected communities may rely upon the printed word for encoding their histories and basic rules of governance, but because of the increased reliance upon the five senses, personal and community memories, the ability to sustain a higher level of accountability in interpersonal relationships, and the need to deal with the consequences of ignoring the information circulating within the cultural and natural ecologies, the abstract systems of representation such as in print and data are less useful. Indeed, as we are witnessing youth become more dependent upon the Internet, there is an increasing alienation between youth who are developing the short-term and immediacy-oriented sense of consciousness and the intergenerational and traditions-oriented knowledge of older generations.

Face-to-face and interdependent communities that carry forward the largely non-monetized traditions of local knowledge and skills, which can also be understood as the cultural commons, are dependent upon language that accurately names the ongoing human/nature relationships. The difference is that the metaphorical language, and the mythopoetic narratives that provide the basic interpretative and moral frameworks, encode the accumulated experience of having learned about the ecology of lived relationships over hundreds—even thousands of years. That is, unlike the abstract language encoded in print that may represent the linguistic colonization of the present by the past (as we see in living by the abstract ideas of Western philosophers and social theorists) as well as in the linguistic colonization of other cultures, language built up over generations of living in one place must provide the conceptual and moral basis for living in ecologically sustainable ways.

In effect, language must carry forward the ability to make explicit past achievements in growing and preparing food, in ceremonies that celebrate the past and living present, the creative arts and craft skills, knowledge of the behavior of local ecosystems, and the achievements and mutual support essential to communities of social justice. It must also carry forward the insights gained from past abuses of other people and the natural environment. An ecologically sustainable use of language must enable the members of the local community to recognize and intergenerationally renew sustainable practices and relationships within both the place-based cultural and natural ecologies. The spoken language thus must meet a very different test—that is, it must contribute to the exercise of ecological intelligence that is both community centered and focused on the long-term prospects of sustainable living. This is very different from the language encoded in print and as data, which is too often lacking in moral accountability and historical accuracy—and is too often imposed by another culture or the elites of the dominant culture.

Face-to-face and intergenerationally connected communities, it needs to be noted, are less vulnerable to the excesses and exploitive practices of the Digital Revolution. As face-to-face communities are less dependent on print-based cultural storage that is so easily exploited, and on collecting massive amounts of data, their members will be less subjected to surveillance by governments and corporations. How do the data collectors operate in environments where electronic communication is less relied upon? How do hackers exploit the wealth of others if the talents, skills, and mentoring that sustain the wealth of the cultural commons are not electronically stored? If the face-to-face communities are focused on local production, and the need for consumerism that contributes to environmental degradation is radically reduced because of the focus on the largely non-monetized cultural commons activities, what would corporations gain from obtaining data profiles on the behaviors and values of people? It should also be noted that face-to-face intergenerationally connected communities that have achieved a degree of self-sufficiency through the exercise of ecological intelligence are also less vulnerable to cyber attacks aimed at disrupting the country's economic and energy infrastructure. They are also better prepared to survive when the breakdown of natural systems leads to chaos within the larger population where the emphasis on individualism has led to a greater dependence upon the money economy where the "survival of the fittest" mentality is likely to take over.

This summary, which takes account of the patterns of communication that sustain the largely non-monetized cultural commons that have a smaller adverse impact on natural systems, is particularly important to being able to recognize how the emerging field of data science and the increased reliance upon algorithms for making decisions across a wide range of cultural life reflects the same Titanic form of consciousness that assumed that relying upon the latest technologies eliminated the need to be aware of environmental perils. In the case of data science and the increased use of algorithms we see a turning away from addressing the cultural/linguistic roots of the ecological crisis, and toward basing decisions on abstractions that, on the surface, promise further progress. It's as though we did not learn anything from how the abstract (that is, culturally context-free) thinking of the major Western philosophers and social theorists' marginalized awareness of other cultural ways of knowing, the legacy of cultural commons knowledge and skills that kept these elite thinkers alive as they wrote their abstract accounts of the nature of ideas, values, the origins of private property, and free markets.

Data science, and innovations in how algorithms can be used to translate the vast amount of data that is a by-product of the near total surveillance culture, represent a revitalization of this cultural tendency to elevate abstract forms of knowledge over the diversity of cultural interpretive frameworks that are the source of personal identities, meanings, memories, patterns of moral reciprocity, lived traditions—some of which should not have been started in the first place. Like the theory of evolution that is now being extended as a way of explaining the better adapted cultural changes (which too often coincide with the political and economic agenda of elite groups), the uses of Big Data and the strategies and policy shifts derived from algorithms are also interpreted through the lens of a taken for granted ideology. It is at the juncture of the digital technologies and the linguistic basis of taken for granted patterns of thinking that we can see the same old colonizing patterns emerging—which continues to be largely unrecognized within educated circles in the West where only the positive characteristics of print are still noted.

As discussed earlier, reducing the emergent, relational, and taken for granted cultural patterns of thinking and behavior (which vary from culture to culture) to what can be encoded in print and as data leads to decisions, strategies, and policy changes that do not take into account local contexts and the lives of the people who will be moved, like figures on a chess board, by elites who think in terms of numbers, correlations, and probabilities. It is important to note how the contributions of data mining and algorithms are impacting the fields of police work, medicine, education, business, economic policies, and the military. Not mentioned by the advocates of data science is how to reduce the level of consumerism and to restore environments so devastated that huge numbers of people are now attempting to migrate across national borders—which is leading to an increasing number of countries erecting fences designed to keep people out. As Vincent Mosco notes, "It is uncertain which is worse: that big data treats problems through oversimplification or that it ignores those that require a careful treatment of subjectivity, including lengthy observation, depth interviews, and an appreciation for the social production of meaning" (2014, 198).

It is important to return to a theme introduced earlier as part of the critique of scientism, especially the taken for granted cultural baggage acquired but not examined as scientists, technologists, engineers, and mathematicians engage in their highly specialized yet culturally uniformed fields of study. As in the past, what was too complex to be reduced to data or to be fully represented in print continues to be ignored. This perpetuates the continued indifference to how what remains of the cultural commons is being undermined by the market system now being given new life by the digital revolution. The current focus on reforming public schools and higher education is unlikely to address the West's proclivity for promoting print-based abstract knowledge and myths such as the idea of the autonomous individual and endless progress, which means that there will be more widespread conflict and social chaos as the ecological crisis deepens. This in turn will continue the cycle downward as marginalized people, particularly among the youth who can no longer believe in the myth of progress, begin to protest their future prospects that will increasingly be marked by droughts, extreme weather, higher levels of unemployment, and the rise of police state tactics. The tragedy will be in the lost possibilities of highly but wrongly educated people being unable to recognize what they do not know—which can partly be attributed to how the print- and now data-based educational process lacks the ability to recognize that all life involves participating in the interdependent cultural and natural ecologies. To recall Thich Nhat Hanh's observation that has particular importance for recognizing the reactionary nature of creating a world of fixed abstractions that can be monetized and politicized without the consent of the people: "impermanence is basic to all forms of life, just as there is no life that exists by itself" (2002, 46–47). The elites promoting the hegemonic technologies of data and print continue to ignore both of these insights.

7

HELPING STEM STUDENTS RECOGNIZE THE POLITICAL CATEGORIES THAT SUPPORT AN ECOLOGICALLY SUSTAINABLE FUTURE

It is impossible to grow up in America without being indoctrinated into accepting the Orwellian reversal of the historically informed meaning of words. Decisions ranging from the Supreme Court to daily media reports continually identify political orientations as either conservative, liberal, socialist, progressive, libertarian, extremist, left and right wing, and so forth. George Orwell's book, *Nineteen Eighty-Four* (1949) was meant as a warning to avoid passively accepting the misuse of a culture's political language, as he understood how changing the meaning of words is a strategy for controlling people's thought and thus political allegiance. To make the point more directly, the Orwellian misuse of our political language leads down the pathway to a totalitarian future. And given how such traditional words as liberal and conservative are being misused, the pathway also leads to the further economic exploitation of the natural systems upon which all life depends.

One of the agendas of STEM reforms is to contribute to a better understanding of the changes occurring in the Earth's natural systems, as well as understanding how cultural practices either contribute to a sustainable future or put the future further at risk. Just as students entering STEM courses have already acquired many of the dominant culture's taken for granted ways of thinking, values, and behaviors, they have also encountered the Orwellian misuse of the basic political vocabulary in nearly all sectors of society. Supreme Court justices who support the agenda of corporations to suppress the power of labor unions as well as gain control of the political process by declaring that corporations, like individuals, can make unlimited contributions to the political candidates are called conservatives. Just as environmentalists and social justice advocates are identified as liberals, even though their agendas include conserving species and habitats, and conserving the rights of the already marginalized to equality in the political, economic, and educational arenas. Advocates of free markets (that is, unrestrained capitalism) that are undermining traditions of community self-sufficiency as well as the prospects of an ecologically sustainable future are labeled as conservatives even though their primary goal is to overturn all cultural traditions, including privacy, that impede their economic goals.

As discussions of the Orwellian language that now dominates the political discourse in America are seldom the focus of sustained discussions in STEM classes, it is important that future scientists acquire a historical perspective on the traditions of thinking, including taken for granted deep cultural assumptions that originally framed the meaning of our political vocabulary. It would seem appropriate for young scientists who are concerned with the loss of habitats and species, as well as the poisoning of natural systems, to identify with the politicians, corporate interests, and think tanks that identify themselves as conservative. Yet they would then be aligning themselves with the groups in denial about the ecological crisis and with unlimited exploitation of natural resources. Similarly, groups concerned with conserving the intergenerational knowledge and skills essential to the cultural commons, as well as conserving the past achievements in the area of social justice too often identify themselves as progressives and liberals even though these labels have traditionally been associated with the idea of the autonomous individual, the progressive nature of change, and the need to overturn traditions.

The following list of political terms are intended to serve as the basis of classroom discussions that will help STEM students recognize when it is necessary to challenge the Orwellian use of language—which may take the form of educating others about the historical meaning of political terms. And even introducing into current discussions the political language that more accurately describes what the political practices should be. Confucius is purported to have suggested that when social relationships begin to break down from misunderstandings it is then necessary to rectify the use of words—that is, to use them in ways that accurately describe areas of differences and agreements. The following effort to rectify the meaning of political terms is historically informed, and is intended to clarify which terminology aligns best with the exercise of ecological intelligence.

Toward a Rectified Political Vocabulary

Environmentalists and proponents of the cultural commons, including the slow food movement and localism practices in general, are more accurately identified as **Bio–Cultural Conservatives**. That is, they recognize the contradictions of conserving species while also identifying with the historical belief systems of liberalism that emphasized change, individualism, a human-centered world, and the backwardness of indigenous cultures.

Social Justice activists, which would include the ACLU, labor unions, as well as groups working to reverse gender, racial, and other forms of discrimination should be identified as **Social Justice Conservatives**. As many have been socialized to think that conservatives are the primary sources of exploitation and discrimination it may be difficult to live with this label. But giving careful attention to the values and assumptions of the sources of exploitation will reveal that those who exploit and exclude others do so primarily for reasons of self-interest, which usually comes down to gaining a political and economic advantage. Also, the past gains in social justice need to be conserved as part of collective memory, which can easily be lost given the ways in which computer-mediated thinking and communication marginalize the importance of long-term memory while reinforcing subjective judgment in a world of seemingly unlimited and context-free data.

Religious groups, given that their core ideas are contained in ancient texts and oral narratives, need to be identified as **Religious Conservatives**. But even this requires greater specificity, such as identifying the various form of religious conservatism in terms of specific traditions, such as **Catholic Conservatism**, **Lutheran Conservatism**, and so forth. The limitations of abstract political labels can partly be overcome by naming specific historical traditions.

As **liberalism** (or **progressivism**) is not a monolithic way of thinking, the various traditions should be identified as fully as possible.

Many **liberal** educators and social justice advocates identify themselves as in the liberal tradition of thinking that is focused on various forms of emancipation from past forms of discrimination, limitations on human freedom, and economic exploitation. The deep cultural assumptions they take for granted include a human-centered view of the world, that critical thinking leads to progress, that the individual is the basic social unit, that both capitalism and traditions are sources of exploitation and limitations on human freedom. Recently, a few educational reformers have become aware of the ecological crisis and are expanding on the idea of an eco-pedagogy. **Social Justice Liberalism** is an accurate way of identifying an ideological tradition that has its roots in Enlightenment thinking— including the failure to distinguish between genuine achievements of the past such as clause 39 of the Magna Carta that provides that each person will have access to a fair trial before a jury of peers, and the many traditions that exploit and marginalize people.

Most individuals and groups now identified as conservatives in the media, by pundits, by otherwise thoughtful academics, and by social justice liberals should be more accurately called **Market Liberals**. They share many of the same deep cultural assumptions with the social justice liberals, such as the progressive nature of change, a human-centered view of the world, that the individual is the basic social unit, and that the entire world should adopt these core assumptions. Additional assumptions not shared with the Social Justice Liberals are derived from the classical liberal theories such as John Locke, Adam Smith, René Descartes, John Stuart Mill, Herbert Spencer, and, now, Milton Friedman. Taken together, these theorists provided the conceptual and moral framework that equates progress with free markets, that justifies the exploitation of the environment and workers, the monetization of traditions, and now with replacing humans or adapting humans to fit the requirements of digital machines.

Current political discourse now refers to **libertarianism** as an ideological orientation that should guide how the role of government is to be understood. It has its roots in the Objectivist theory of Ayn Rand. Her main ideas include the following: that individuals should use reason to make decisions that advance their self-interest, that the role of government should be limited to enforcing contacts and providing for national defense, that the values of empathy and altruism represent a conspiracy on the part of the weak and unsuccessful against the strong, that the role of government is not to redistribute wealth in ways that compensate for the failures and weakness of individuals, that unrestrained capitalism leads to progress and that the strong and competitive deserve material success. Missing from her thinking, and from that of today's followers, is an awareness of environmental limits, an understanding of the systemic reasons that limit being able to escape from poverty, and the unfairness of the current distribution of wealth and power that make democracy little more than an empty slogan that hides the real sources of injustice.

The need to use the dominant political language in ways that lead to clarity about the values and beliefs of each position requires the following qualifications. There are people and groups that believe that traditions do not and thus should not be changed. They are not conservatives in the Edmund Burke or Wendell Berry sense of the term, and while many of these traditionalists identify with different forms of religious fundamentalism, there are others that share the absolute and unchanging principles that guide the market liberals and libertarians. They should be identified as **Traditionalists**. This is the term that represents people who are unaware that all traditions, as cultural constructs, undergo changes—with some changes occurring more slowly than others.

Individuals and social groups such as the Ku Klux Klan and other neo-fascist groups should be called **Extremists** or **Reactionary**.

There is, overall, the need to avoid using political terms such as conservative when words such as "caution" and "thoughtfulness" convey a more accurate description. The non-reflective overuse of the word conservative leads to a general state of confusion that marginalizes the growing importance, in light of the ecological crisis and what is being overturned by the digital revolution, of being aware of the ecologically and community sustainable traditions that need to be intergenerationally renewed—that is, conserved.

Questions to be Discussed by Students

These questions need to be modified by the STEM teacher in ways that take account of the background experience, including ethnicity, of the students.

1   Edward Shils, the author of *Tradition*, makes the point that science is an "anti-tradition tradition." In what way is he correct? Is adherence to the scientific method a tradition? Are the vocabularies that scientists take for granted also examples of traditions? But in what ways do the sciences overturn traditions?

Are the traditions that are overturned by scientific knowledge always expressions of superstitions?

Can you identify traditions overturned by scientific knowledge, and the resulting technologies, that represent important past achievement? Is privacy an example of the latter? What are other examples of intergenerational knowledge within your ethnic group that are being overturned by technologies derived from scientific discoveries?

2   The above questions bring into focus that science not only leads to genuine gains in understanding and in the quality of life, but it also leads to the loss of traditions that are still valued by people—which range from food issues, craft knowledge, moral narratives, to social justice traditions. Is science inherently supportive of democracies, or do other cultural values come into play when scientific advances serve the interests of elite groups while at the same time undermining local democracy? What are examples of other cultural influences that lead scientists to bypass the democratic process?

3   Do environmental scientists align most closely with the political tradition of conservatism or with liberalism? (The teacher should list the core beliefs and assumptions of the two traditions of thinking—as well as point out that the core values and assumptions of classical liberalism were derived from Western philosophers.) After the genuine achievements that were gained from liberal theorists are discussed, ask the students if these social justice achievements become what then needs to be intergenerationally renewed—that is, conserved.

4   A difficult question: If natural and cultural ecologies are characterized by being emergent, relational, and co-dependent (that is, no fixed and independent entities), which political tradition is less likely to recognize local ecologies and, instead, to base political decisions on the belief that there are universal Truths such as the autonomous individual, free markets, and progress?

5   How do different ideologies influence what scientists regard as legitimate research? Which ideologies are used to justify scientific research that underlies the digital revolution, the conservation of species and habitats, the genetic modification of plants and animals, the creation of new surveillance technologies and weapons systems?

8

HOW STEM TEACHERS CAN ADDRESS THE FEAR AND ECOLOGICAL UNCERTAINTIES BY INTRODUCING STUDENTS TO THE DIFFERENCES BETWEEN WISDOM AND DATA

Scientists are very good at explaining the changes occurring in natural systems, but when it comes to addressing which changes in cultural values and lifestyles will slow the degradation of natural systems they are strangely silent beyond suggesting anything more than we should not pollute and that we should adopt new environmental policies at the national level. In effect, they gear their comments to what they think politicians need to hear. Living in the Monterey area of California for the last few years has given me the opportunity to observe the interactions between scientists (especially marine scientists) and the general public. One presentation stands out as a problem that STEM graduates must be prepared to address as they interact with their students and members of the community. Following a clear and data-based explanation of the rate at which oceans are becoming more acidic, and the rate at which coral systems are dying and the marine food webs are being threatened, a person in the audience asked the scientist what she could do to address the problem. As she put it, "can anything be done to reverse the rate of acidification?" The marine biologist, who had testified before Congress, responded by saying that someone will figure it out. Her question was motivated by a real concern about the impact of the ecological crisis on the lives she cared about.

Similarly, as droughts and extreme weather become more widespread, and as scientists (including classroom science teachers) report on further changes in the life-supporting characteristics of natural systems, people's fears (including those of students) will become more intense—especially as they are now witnessing on a near daily basis how wars and environmental disasters are turning more people into refugees crossing national borders in search of safety and the basic necessities of life. In short, as there is no evidence that the melting of glaciers will be reversed, that rapidly depleted fish stocks are recovering, that ocean levels are beginning to fall, and that species and habitats are recovering, future scientific reports will further undermine the idea that a life of continued economic prosperity will continue to expand.

Fear and a sense of helplessness—especially among students who are thinking what the future holds for them—will become more widespread. The classroom science teacher needs to offer more than generalities that things are not as bad as being reported in the media, and that experts will find the answers as they have in the past. The evidence of ecological changes, as well as social justice issues still not addressed, are based on data and the predictions now being made by the data scientists. The form of science described in earlier chapters as scientism, where the scientist's established reputation in an area of scientific research becomes the basis for suggesting fundamental changes in cultural practices, needs to be avoided. STEM teachers need to avoid stepping into the quagmire of scientism by introducing students to the scientism of a noted scientist such as Michio Kaku who claims that "all the technological revolutions described here are leading to a single point: the creation of a planetary civilization" (2011, 327). What is there to fear on the part of students, as Kaku's vision promises a future in something really grand: a planetary civilization? To recall the other examples of scientism, there is E.O. Wilson's claim that as the major religions of the world represented the adaptive earlier behaviors of cultures shrouded in ignorance, but with an understanding of Darwin's theory of natural selection, religions should now be abandoned—with these cultures adopting natural selection as the guiding force governing all forms of life (1998, 264). His statement that "science for its part will test relentlessly every assumption about the human condition and in time uncover the bedrock of the moral and religious sentiments" (265) is also shared by computer scientists such as Gregory Stock, Ray Kurzweil, and Eric Schmidt (remember the sub-title of his book, *Reshaping the Future of People, Nations and Business*), as well as those working in labs to create algorithms that will replace human decision making, by molecular biologists such as Lee Silver who proposed in *Remaking Eden* (2007) that scientists should create gene-rich species of humans who will manage the symbolic world, by Stephen Hawking who claimed that when we have the mathematical formula that accounts for the theory of everything we will know why we are here, and Carl Sagan who wants the culture's highest rewards given to scientists who "convincingly disprove established beliefs" (1997, 35). Sagan did not qualify what he meant by established beliefs; rather the mission of science is to hold all beliefs to meeting the narrow epistemological standard of scientists—which is a repeat of the Promethean role Wilson assigns to scientists. None of these expressions of scientism addresses what the students need to learn about changes in cultural practices that slow the rate of environmental change—and most important of all, how to revitalize or form new communities that are less dependent upon the industrial system that will be weakened by the environmental changes or by cyber attacks.

As pointed out earlier, how scientists intervene in natural ecologies, over time affects what happens in the cultural ecologies. Thus, crossing from legitimate scientific research and development into the domain of culture, where the boundaries are made less clear by how the scientist's own core taken for granted ideas and values are derived from the linguistic ecology inherited from the past, means that scientism is a constant problem. Also, as pointed out earlier, scientists and others working in STEM related fields have made genuine contributions thus making some forms of scientism both inevitable and even life enhancing. We do not live in an either/or world, with clearly delineated borders. The use of print (which is a culture changing technology) has led to many unintended consequences, with many of them leading to benefits that outweigh their more destructive impacts—though the jury is still out. But there are examples of scientism that are clearly destructive. The scientism that led to giving the Nazi agenda scientific legitimacy by justifying it on the basis of Social Darwinism was criminal in the worst sense. And the scientism that combines data with the market liberal ideology that is replacing humans with machines and algorithms that is undermining local democracy, and that further replaces both face-to-face and intergenerational relationships with sitting in front of a computer screen, may prove over the long term to be equally destructive.

The Mediating Role of STEM Teachers as the Ecological Crisis Challenges the Myth of Progress

A basic reality that STEM teachers cannot ignore: namely, that the digital revolution is producing profound changes in the world's cultures. What is unique about these changes is that they are embraced by many people ranging from scientists, business women and men, educators, average citizens, and just about everybody else who values convenience, instantaneousness, multiple forms of empowerment, and the ability to escape from face-to-face relationships into the seemingly boundless and abstract world of information and data. The combination of surveillance technologies—connectivity, multiple monitoring systems, and storage—bring all aspects of the natural world as well as cultural life under the new god of capitalism and data-based decision making. Quickly disappearing from human memory are the various mythologically centered sources of ultimate authority that provided an integrated and morally coherent world view, and were renewed through rituals, ceremonies, and narratives—and in many instances prescribed the punishment fitted to different moral transgressions. Also disappearing are the narratives of past social justice achievements, such as when the voices of the people began to hold in check authoritarian leaders, when the exploitation of child labor began to be challenged, when workers began to organize in order to achieve social justice in the workplace, and so forth. The narratives about past artistic achievements, and the emergence of an environmental ethic, are disappearing as more attention is given to "objective" information and data. Indeed, historical memory of both the destruction done to others as well as of the higher expressions of intelligence and moral accountability are also being seen as irrelevant in today's data-driven world.

While this new god of data, and its new priesthood, has not totally displaced the God of the Old and New Testaments, its emphasis on the authority of data is bringing about fundamental changes in the vocabulary various cultures used in the past to carry forward their wisdom traditions. For those closest to the center of this digital revolution, the word wisdom is seldom if ever used. When Bill Gates, an early prophet of this new religion, is purported to have claimed that we need to recover wisdom, few people would have understood what the word previously referred to, and what it might mean in the modern world where data is understood as eliminating subjective judgments and interpretations based on archaic moral narratives. The vision of 17th- and 18th-century Enlightenment philosophers is at last being realized by how computer scientists are now putting decision making on a supposedly objective basis that relies upon data. By ignoring the social construction of objective knowledge, information, and now data it is possible to transcend entirely the murky realm of politics that is still influenced by memory and values derived from the pre-scientific world of ancient religious narratives.

Those who refuse to recognize the final authority of data are still looking through a glass darkly. Their archaic mindset leads to raising questions that cannot be objectively answered—such as the differences between wisdom and data. Taking the differences seriously would require entering a realm already colonized by the followers of the scientific method who have demonstrated the power to predict the behavior of particles moving through space. The astonishing achievements of scientists suggest that we do not need to understand wisdom. What can wisdom help us understand if science has given us the ability to land men on the moon, and to genetically alter the basis of different forms of life? Besides, understanding wisdom first requires understanding the diversity of how humans have understood the nature and sources of wisdom. And what citizen of the Digital Age can take time away from keeping up with the Tweets, cell phone and e-mail messages from friends and employers who expect their employees to be continually connected? And who is interested in entering the rabbit hole of human history chronicled by the winners, and who is genuinely concerned that the abstract world of data misrepresents the emergent, relational, and co-dependent life-sustaining processes in the natural and cultural ecologies within which we live? Isn't it enough that data can be used to reveal trend lines in profits, the expansion or reduction in crime rates, and the rate of acidification of the world oceans?

There is no question that the abstract world of data is genuinely useful even when it represents a formulaic response that hides the many limitations both in what data is supposed to represent—and in the moral issues seldom recognized in the political decisions surrounding its use. As the above sentences suggest, moving outside the certainties of an objective and measurable world also requires understanding that one's thinking is based on culturally specific taken for granted assumptions about how to understand reality. That this culturally constructed world is assumed to be composed of fixed entities such as autonomous individuals, abstract ideas and values that are both objective and have universal status, and that the life force called progress is like a road sign pointing the direction the rest of the world is to follow.

Recognizing the conceptual foundations of one's taken for granted cultural assumptions seems like an unnecessary detour when data is so easy to understand. This would require more than historical knowledge. That is, it would require a knowledge of one's own culture as well as that of other cultures—especially those that recognized that the emergent, relational, and co-dependent world within which they live are the basis of sustainable forms of ecological intelligence. For the typical citizen of the emerging digital culture, this effort would seem a waste of time as a new class of experts, the data scientists, as well as algorithms (and the computer scientists, programmers, and engineers working behind the scenes to create autonomous algorithms) possess the form of intelligence that easily turns data into decisions.

The Challenge that Data Poses for STEM Teachers

Before discussing why wisdom is needed in a world that increasingly relies on data-based decision making, as well as how data misrepresents the world in which we live, it needs to be acknowledged that for all its limitations data is useful in providing a better understanding of patterns, trend lines, casual relationships, rates of change, and changes in effectiveness and efficiency. It provides, in many instances, a more accurate account of the behavior of social and natural systems that might otherwise be misrepresented by a lack of close attention, and by efforts to hide the shortcomings in human behavior. For example, without data we have to rely upon conjectures and traditional misconceptions about the behavior of marine ecosystems. Data provides a more accurate understanding of how many sharks are being killed each year in order to satisfy a traditional cultural preference for shark fin soup. Similarly, data provides a more accurate understanding of how fraudulent Medicare and Social Security claims are distorting the national budget. Data is also useful in providing an expanded understanding of other cultural patterns of behavior relating to gender and racial discrimination, and so forth.

In spite of its many uses, data, like the scientific method, tells us "what is" within a limited context. It does not tell us how we "ought" to respond to the issues and problems revealed by the "what is" information. In order to understand the limitations of data and the role of cultural influences that are largely ignored due to an over estimation of the authority that has been conferred on data, it is necessary to take account of the following:

1   Like print, taken for granted cultural assumptions influence both what is regarded as important to represent in the form of data, as well as the interpretation of how it is to be used. That is, while data is assumed to be objective, there is always a decision made by an individual or group about what is to be measured and represented as data. This decision is culturally influenced because

the thinking and values of the decision makers are influenced by the languaging processes that tacitly reproduce earlier cultural ways of thinking and valuing. Data represents only a segment, like a snapshot, of what is emergent, relational, and co-dependent within the larger ecological systems. What it represents, like René Magritte's famous painting "Ceci n'est pas une pipe" is only a partial abstract and symbolic image—and not the pipe itself. In short, data is only a surface representation, and it encodes the taken for granted cultural assumptions that are at the front end, the initial decisions that guide the data gathering process.

2   How the data is interpreted is also a culturally influenced process. The mindset of the individual and group interpreting the data in terms of what it means is always under the influence of the cultural assumptions that are taken for granted. For example, the environmental scientist brings a different set of assumptions and values to the process of interpreting the data than that of the data scientists working for a corporation or an office of education concerned with acquiring "objective" evidence of learning outcomes (to use the jargon). What the myth of objective data requires overlooking is the ecology of linguistic influences, the ecology of identities, and the ecology of interpretative and moral frameworks that are variously called an ideology, the scientific method, and the individual's critical rationality. The cultural/linguistic ecology that influences both ends of the data collecting and interpreting process is an inescapable aspect of the interpreted world in which we live. That we can escape into a world of objective facts, data, and the printed word is a modern myth.

3   Because the surface and momentary measurement or observation of a phenomenon does not take into account its larger dynamic context, and because many Westerners carry forward the Cartesian tradition of thinking of themselves as rational spectators of an inert, material, external world, data (as well as print) reinforces a basic ontological misconception about a world of permanent, fixed, and Platonic universal entities. Those who claim to have a rational and thus objective understanding of this abstract world too often possess power and authority over those who acknowledge they live in an impermanent and interpreted world.

4   The ideology that serves as an interpretive framework for determining the meaning and uses of data reinforces an instrumental moral framework that, with the exceptions of how environmentalists use data, serves the interests of market liberals who promote consumerism and the monetization of everyday life. This instrumental moral framework is supported by the cultural assumptions about the autonomy of the individual and the importance of progress in producing material wealth and in exploiting the environment.

It would not be too much of a stretch to claim that the dominant Anglo/European print-based culture, out of ignorance of its own modernizing assumptions, uses data as though it legitimates the decisions that lead to further economic progress. That is, data is being viewed as providing both an account of "what is" as well as what "ought to be." Actually, what is represented as data is too limited, and too much a reflection of the assumptions of the experts setting the data gathering process in motion, to provide the moral guidelines for how it is to be used. The moral and instrumental guidelines are derived, instead, from the prevailing taken for granted ideology of the social groups seeking legitimation for their decisions. If this were recognized, the ideology of the group masking their policy decisions, including the justifications for replacing people with machines, might be challenged more often.

But how many people have been educated to recognize how certain words in the vocabulary, such as "objective," "rational," "progress," "expert," "science," and now "data," are assumed to represent certainties that are beyond political debate. The irony is that when judged in terms of the past decisions of the ideologically driven groups who have relied on data to justify their economic and political agendas—in promoting technological innovations, in monetizing the cultural commons, in colonizing other cultures, and in educating the country's youth to equate success and happiness with climbing the pyramid of consumerism and wasteful living—data-based decision making has been both de-humanizing as well as ecologically destructive. Indeed, data has become the common currency shared within the interlocking surveillance technologies that are putting the country on the road to a techno-fascist and capitalistic future.

If current market and individually centered ideologies are accelerating environmental changes that are leading, as some scientists now claim, to the sixth extinction of life on this planet, then the question about the recovery of wisdom becomes not only more relevant, but more urgent. When we consider not only the wisdom traditions within different cultures, but also how these traditions were influenced by profoundly different cultural mythologies/epistemologies, centuries of learning how to encode their guiding moral frameworks in narratives, dance, and in every aspect of their cultural commons, as well as in their relationships with the natural world, the question becomes more urgent. That is, will knowledge of the wisdom traditions of other cultures lead to fundamental changes in the Western mindset in time to avert the social chaos and ecological endgame that lies just decades ahead? In spite of my increasing doubts that the majority of academics and experts guiding a variety of innovative agendas will take seriously the challenge of basing decisions on wisdom rather than data, I will nevertheless identify a number of wisdom traditions that still guide human/nature relationships—and from which groups on the fringes of our mainstream individualistic, consumer-dependent, and profit-oriented culture are learning. Hopefully, STEM teachers will also recognize when they need to remind students to consider when wisdom rather than data should guide their decisions. The following represent some of the wisdom traditions that students can learn from—especially now that the deepening ecological crises reduces the margin for human error which is too often expression of hubris and mythical thinking. The wisdom traditions of Buddhism and Confucianism that were discussed earlier need to be considered again—particularly as their wisdom about relationships was not derived either from the West's scientific method or from data. Rather, both became wisdom traditions by giving careful attention to what constitutes moral and spiritual relationships with others, and to holding in check the mix of negative psychological and cultural forces that lead to competition and fault-finding of others. Given what has been discussed about the limitations of scientism, a second reading, with ongoing class discussions, will lead to a deeper understanding of a whole realm of cultural developments that lie beyond the field of the sciences and technologies.

Two Ancient Relationally Oriented Wisdom Traditions: Buddhism and Confucianism

The fundamental differences between the cultural patterns reinforced by data-based storage, thinking, and communication can be seen by comparing the difference between what the Buddhists call the Path, and what they refer to as "wandering about"—which refers to the lifestyle that is not reflective and is continually influenced by outside forces and shifting subjective whims. The lifestyle of "wandering about" is exemplified in the West as a consumer-driven lifestyle and the many illnesses that accompany it. It is also reinforced by how the Internet reinforces change, short attention spans and memory, and an instrumental approach to information and data. A critical question to consider is: Given that much of the communication with the Other is through iPhones, social media such as Facebook, and through Internet sites inviting a response to what the Other has written—and that is most often a response to the Other you know only in terms of what is written—how likely is it to be guided by the mindfulness characteristic of Buddhism's Path of eight steps that lead to moral reciprocity in human relationships? How do the multiple non-verbal patterns of communication that are part of face-to-face relations, and which are not driven by stereotypes and hatred for the Other, moderate what and how the Other is brought into the communication process? Is Martin Buber's distinction between I-Thou and I-It patterns, where the Other is an object to be manipulated, another way of understanding how Buddhism avoids treating the Other as an object? The I-Thou relationship, which does not prejudge the Other, involves responding to who they are in that moment. What is important to consider is whether Internet mediated communication fosters the development and maturity of character that consistently seeks what constitutes what is morally right in the different relationships that Buddhism identifies as the Path.

In considering the Path's eight steps—(1) Right views, (2) Right Intent, (3) Right Speech, (4) Right Conduct, (5) Right Livelihood, (6) Right Effort, (7) Right Mindfulness, (8) Right Concentration (Smith, 1991, 105–112)—how does the response of the Others contribute to the state of mindfulness, rather than to the "hurry-up and let's get on to what I am really interested in" mentality so prominent in the West? It is notable that possessing the right amount of data is not included as contributing to the path of mindfulness, nor are speed and efficiency what govern relationships. As the behavioral and thought process associated with each of these steps is elaborated upon, it becomes clear that Buddhism is focused on the moral and spiritual dimensions of relationships as they are experienced in a constantly changing world. It is also clear that the Path requires a lifelong commitment, which differs radically from the short attention span and expectation of obtaining instantaneous results reinforced by cyberspace experiences. Perhaps more important in terms of the need to reduce the human impact on natural systems, the Path represents an alternative to the consumer-dependent lifestyle valued in the West. It is also important to note that different traditions of Buddhism are being taken seriously in the West, but not in sufficient numbers to have a real impact on the still growing influence of the digital revolution that supports the global expansion of the market system.

Confucianism, like Buddhism, is also a religion so deeply ingrained in daily cultural practices that it is understood more as the taken for granted reality of daily life. Its fivefold principles also challenge the individually centered and efficiency-oriented mindset reinforced by the Internet culture. They include the following: **Jen** which "involves simultaneously a feeling of humanity toward others and respect for oneself, an indivisible sense of the dignity of life wherever it appears." **Chun tzu** highlights relationships that are the opposite of the competitive, petty, and ego-centered person. The person of Chun tzu puts others at ease and engages in what Martin Buber later referred to as I-Thou relationships and dialogue. **Li** is the quality that leads to doing things correctly—in the use of language, in avoiding extremes, in the correct ordering of relationships within the family and society. **Te** is the power of moral examples that attract the willing support of the people. **Wen** refers to the "arts of peace," specifically the power of the arts to transform human nature in ennobling ways (Smith, 1991, 175–181). Again, there is no mention of the importance of data in these life guiding principles. And the principles, unlike the Eightfold Path I identified earlier as promoting both individual self interest and the economic agenda in the West, lack both the messianic drive to colonize others and to promote an economy that is overshooting environmental limits. Unfortunately, the digital revolution, which is central to economic growth in China and other cultures with a Confucian past, is having a transformative impact on the youth of these cultures.

A critical issue is whether the wisdom traditions of Buddhism and Confucianism will survive as the mindset of the youth of these cultures is being shaped by the Westernizing mindset of the digital revolution. The relational wisdom of both Buddhism and Confucianism were intergenerationally renewed though face-to-face communication, through mentoring, and through being aware that others take for granted these principles as moral imperatives. The spread of market forces, rising material standards of living, slick media images connecting consumerism with individual happiness, the role of the digital revolution in expanding the economies of Asian countries and in Westernizing their approaches to education, all work against youth even being aware of these ancient wisdom traditions—except to view them as the old and pre-modern ways of their grandparents.

Ecologically Informed Wisdom Traditions that are Sources of Resistance to the Individually Centered, Consumer-dependent, and Data-based Culture

It is especially important for STEM teachers to understand that the ecologically informed wisdom traditions that stand in sharp contrast to the Western mindset that is making a cult of data-based decisions, and that have the most relevance for learning how to live less environmentally destructive lives, represent the achievements of many of the world's indigenous cultures. Their wisdom was not acquired from abstract thinkers such as Western philosophers, nor was it acquired from books and from data. Rather, it was acquired from living in one place over hundreds even thousands of years, giving close attention to the cycles and patterns of interdependencies of life in the natural world, using myths as repositories of practical ecologically informed knowledge, narratives and ceremonies that connected the generations in webs of meaning, rituals around food and healing practices, and renewing the knowledge and moral insights learned by previous generations by taking account of the ongoing changes in the local bioregion. What seems common to these wisdom traditions is that unlike the mythic account of "man's" fall in the second chapter of the *Book of Genesis*, and the injunction to name and subordinate the plants and animals to human will, they learned from nature itself; that is, the "Garden of Eden," to stay with that metaphor. That is, rather than escaping from the Garden by creating a human-centered world of moral and conceptual dichotomies and categories, the indigenous cultures engaged in what is today known as biomimicry, which shows up in their metaphorical language and their knowledge of local ecosystems.

Giving close attention to the information flowing within and between the natural systems, such as how the behavior of animals, even that of the tree, anticipates the severity of the coming winter, fosters reliance upon the exercise of ecological intelligence. Awareness of the interconnected patterns in a world of impermanence, as well as awareness that adapting how to meet human needs in ways that take account of these changing patterns is essential to sustaining life within the biotic/human community, is profoundly different from surface, abstract, snap-shot images we call data that is supposed to enable students to construct their own knowledge.

There is no sense of the sacred in the world reproduced as data, and there is no awareness of an inclusive spirituality. Without a sense of the sacred and an inclusive spirituality, everything becomes possible to the mindset that reduces the cultural and natural ecologies to data, including destroying forests, mountains, streams and rivers, and their multiple animal inhabitants if it leads to more profits and human convenience. It's only a matter of a change in what is regarded as a moral consensus that now holds scientists in check from genetically engineering changes in human life—as they are already at work genetically engineering animals to fit more efficiently into the food production processes.

The mythic thinking of the peoples who have inhabited the South American Andes for centuries, and whose understanding of Pachamama as the force that nurtures humans as humans nurture nature, has led to one of the world's megadiversities of edible plants. It also represents many of the elements of wisdom shared by other indigenous cultures. As explained by Grimaldo Rengifo Vasquez,

> In the Andean world everything is alive and important; nothing is inert and nothing is superfluous. The very stone is alive, it speaks and the peasant converses with it as person to person. It is not that the peasant extends the notion of a person to the stone (which is generally understood as 'personification') but rather that, for the peasant, the stone is alive—possessing the attributes of the *runa* and vice versa.
>
> In the Andean context we cannot speak either of the inanimate as opposed to the animate, or of the essential as opposed to the contingent. The whole *Pacha* is a community of interconnected living beings, in which man and water are as important and alive as are the *buacas* (dieties) and the wind in terms of the regeneration of life.
>
> (Apffel-Marglin, 1998, 97)

During my visit to Cajamarca, the site of Pizarro's capture and execution of Atahualpa, the sovereign emperor of the Inca empire, my Western consciousness was opened up to how the stone could be understood as being alive, and an active participant in the information networks that connected all forms of life in the bioregion to the cosmos. My Western consciousness, oriented toward actions that increased efficiency and a humanly controlled world, led to wondering why the stones were not used as boundary markers as in England, France, and other Western countries. Instead they lay scattered across the field. Following the advice to pick up a stone, I found how its surface appearance indicates the level of moisture in the soil—which is vital information for the farmer to understand. The number of eggs a bird lays, the number of animals in a herd—even the condition of their fur, and so forth—are signs of the current and forthcoming patterns operating in the regeneration of life. In effect, the wisdom carried forward from earlier centuries among the Andean peoples is that everything communicates, everything is part of the same spiritual and moral universe, and that these cycles of interdependence should not be broken. But they now are being broken as Western extraction industries are tearing up the Earth for oil, gold, and other resources needed to produce the throw-away, data-driven culture of the West.

The wisdom of the Aboriginal peoples that mapped and storied what we now call Australia for 40 to 50 thousand years also avoids the anthropocentrism of the tribal cultures that eventually put their narratives in print that we now read as the *Book of Genesis*. As recounted by Robert Lawlor in the *Voices of the First Day: Awakening in the Aboriginal Dreamtime* (1991) their cosmology was also the basis of their moral order, the source of the wisdom that guided their uses of technologies, and resulted in a level of ecological intelligence that far surpassed the Anglo culture that invaded the land and set out to Westernize them. Lawlor summarizes the wisdom that was integral to their cosmology in the following way:

> All creatures—from stars to humans to insects—share in the consciousness of the primary creative force, and each, in its own ways, mirrors a form of that consciousness. In this sense the Dreamtime stories perpetuate a unified worldview. This unity compelled the Aborigines to respect and adore the earth as if it were a book imprinted with the mystery of the original creation. The goal of life was to preserve the earth as much as possible, in its initial purity. The subjugation and domestication of plants and animals and all the other manipulation and exploitation of the natural world—the basis of Western civilization and 'progress'—were antithetical to the sense of a common consciousness and origin shared by every creature and equally with the creators. To exploit this integrated world as to do the same to oneself.
>
> (Lawlor, 1991, 17)

The cosmologies of the Quechua, the Australian Aborigine, as well as many other indigenous cultures recognized a sacred and thus moral order that was (and is) profoundly different from the instructions in the *Book of Genesis* for man to name the creatures of God's creation and to take control of them. What is often not recognized is that the *Bible* was written by a tribal culture dedicated to a cosmology and moral order centered on a monotheistic God, and the surrounding cultures that understood all forms of life as sacred and animated by different spirits, and thus as participants in the same spiritual universe, were regarded as challenging the one true God. The irony is that these first indigenous cultures were initially pursuing the path leading to ecological wisdom, while the author of the *Book of Genesis* (believed to be Moses) was laying the conceptual and moral foundations for the anthropocentic culture of the West, which would later become the foundation for the industrial and capitalist exploitation of nature. This anthropocentric cosmology, as well as early Biblical instructions to take control of the Earth and to multiply (both now contributing to the ecological catastrophe we are now entering), continues as the basis of today's emphasis on progress that now relies so heavily on data-based decisions.

The youth of indigenous cultures, from the Salishan, Haida, Dene, Inuit, to thousands of other indigenous cultures spread around the world, are now caught between their ancient ecologically informed sources of wisdom and the modern world of the supposedly autonomous individual that is dependent upon consumerism and the abstractions appearing on computer screens. Even the tensions between the time tested forms of wisdom and the convenience and the immediate access to the data generated by experts whose long-range goal is to replace as much of what is human with robots and machine forms of intelligence are disappearing as the word wisdom is not part of the vocabularies of scientism and the digital culture.

Where in the narratives of the computer scientists, data scientists, heads of corporations, agencies protecting the nation's security, and all the other individuals and groups who have now made data the highest form of knowledge, do we find any concerns about the lack of ecologically informed wisdom articulated in the above observations about what is being lost? The most abstract, that is context free, bits of information that are constructed on the basis of some expert's taken for granted cultural assumptions, who is often working for others higher up in the systems of economic and human exploitation, are supposed to guide decisions that will impact people's lives—people who are largely unaware of the shortcomings of data and the various market-oriented ideologies that guide its use. One of the great ironies of our times is that the traditions of ecologically informed wisdom are relegated to marginal status in our systems of higher education; that is, to anthropology courses that enable students to understand the backwardness of these pre-rational cultures still guided by storytelling myths.

The other irony, for which people will experience a new depth of human suffering when the ecological systems begin to collapse, is that the possibility of finding from within our own Western cultures the basis of an ecologically or even relationally informed wisdom tradition is being undermined by the values and knowledge given high status in our public schools and universities. As I observed in an earlier book, *The Culture of Denial* (1997) the high status knowledge promoted in higher education is largely print-based and thus abstract, and increasingly computer mediated. It is also ideologically framed by the misconceptions of the 17th- and 18th-century Enlightenment thinkers who promoted overturning traditions by relying upon critical thinking, scientific knowledge, and a secular worldview. Critical thinking and scientific knowledge continue to lead to important advances, particularly in addressing social justice issues, but the abstract thinking of the Enlightenment thinkers led them to ignore such important traditions as the guilds that served as community centered systems of mutual support, and the many forms of intergenerational knowledge essential to living less monetized lives.

At the core of the high status knowledge promoted in higher education are the deep cultural assumptions about the autonomous nature of the individual, a mechanistic and human centered (anthropocentric) world, the progressive nature of change, the combination of cultural hubris and missionary spirit that justifies colonizing other cultures to adopt the core features of the Western mindset that now accepts the replacement of humans, along with their traditions, with digital machines. Given these characteristics of high status knowledge, and the increasing reliance upon computer-mediated thinking and as sources of entertainment, there is little likelihood that either students or their professors will even be aware of the relational wisdom of Buddhism and Confucianism. They will also ignore the ecologically informed wisdom traditions of indigenous cultures that are becoming increasingly aware of how Western cultures are accelerating global changes that are threatening their future existence.

In spite of the continuing imprint of the anthropocentric message in the *Book of Genesis* on the consciousness of most Jews, Christians (especially fundamentalist Christians), and even the growing atheist movement that continues to adhere to more of the Judaic/Christian cosmology than they recognize, there are other obstacles to acquiring a shared wisdom tradition that would limit the excesses inherent in the libertarian/market liberal ideology that relies upon data to justify everyday decisions. Unlike many of the indigenous cultures that developed over the centuries ecologically informed wisdom traditions, and embedded this wisdom in the many dimensions of their symbolic culture that guided daily practices, the West's guiding modernizing cosmology is interpreted from the perspectives of the many tribal traditions that have been melded into what is called Western civilization—which is a high-status phrase that hides the tribal roots of various groups that occupied the territories we now call England, France, Italy, Poland, and so forth. Again, it's a matter of so-called autonomous individuals and their primary tribal roots being overwhelmed by the libertarian/market liberal myth of the role that data plays in achieving even more material progress.

There are writers such as Henry David Thoreau, Aldo Leopold, Rachel Carson, and Wendell Berry who provide key sensitivities and insights upon which a wisdom tradition could be based. Whether youth will encounter their writings as they search the Internet or encounter them in the educational software written by the technologically minded programmers is problematic. And if they were to read any of them, each student would need to make her/his own decision about taking them seriously when the consumer-oriented cultural ecology that impinges on their senses and behaviors communicates a different message: namely, that consumerism is still the main road to personal happiness and success. Data is the basis of this message, as well as the innovations that keep the economy expanding even as it shrinks the opportunities to work in settings not dictated by the digital systems.

The final blow to a wisdom tradition becoming the primary moral guide that leads to reflecting on whether data-based decision making takes into account the primary responsibilities to the natural and cultural ecologies upon which we depend is that few people, even those who are highly educated, understand what is problematic about the origins and uses of data. It has now acquired a cult standing, which will only be strengthened as the digital revolution expands its influence over more aspects of daily life.

The final judgment is that the robust ecologically informed wisdom traditions that once guided how to live within the limits and possibilities of the local bioregions have now been largely overwhelmed. The central question today is whether the increasing emphasis on data and reliance upon new digital technologies will lead to an awareness that one of the central messages in the *Book of Genesis*, which is, "Be fruitful, and multiply, and replenish the earth, and subdue it: and have **dominion** over the fish of the sea, and over the fowl of the air, and over everything that moveth upon the earth" is leading to the collapse of the ecosystems upon which we depend (Genesis 1:28, italics added).

As computer scientists have announced that the transition to the age of singularity is now occurring, and that super-intelligent computers will take over as the world enters the post-biological phase of evolution, it will be up to computers to interpret what "dominion" means, and find in their world of seemingly endless data the moral guide lines that will replace the ecological wisdom of the indigenous cultures that were long-term inhabitants of the land. Perhaps the next exodus should be from the Garden of Data and its tree of knowledge.

Questions for Students to Consider

1   Ask students to review what is important about relying upon data to justify decisions that address environmental and social issues. What are the potential limitations in decision making that a reliance upon data helps to overcome? Also discuss the different problems that arise when data becomes the primary basis for decision making.

2   Also, review the forms of knowledge that are lost when behaviors are reduced to data. What are the cultural/linguistic processes that are ignored when it is assumed that data represents an objective account of a behavior within a natural and cultural system? Also, review what students see as the limitations of data when the natural and cultural ecologies are characterized as emergent, relational, and co-dependent. Students should also review why impermanence better describes every aspect of the world they live in rather than permanence, fixed identities and qualities. Also, have them discuss why the reliance upon English nouns misrepresents the emergent, relational, and co-dependent world that can be described as natural and cultural ecologies.

3   Given that the environmental sciences focus on the behaviors of ecological systems, and views them as emergent, relational, and co-dependent semiotic systems, what is there about the traditions of scientific knowledge that failed to develop the wisdom traditions that are so common among indigenous cultures? Have students Google Jeannette Armstrong's You Tube talk on the Doctrine of Discovery (www.**youtube**.com/watch?v=5iHuYQpiq84). Her description of Salishan ecological intelligence includes essential aspects of scientific knowledge, but also combines how this knowledge is turned into intergenerational wisdom by being incorporated into the symbolic aspects of the cultures—such as narratives, ceremonies, creative arts, appropriate technologies, and face-to-face traditions of mutual support.

4   Ask students to consider and document when possible the wisdom traditions of the indigenous cultures that occupied the land where their communities now exist. Also, ask them to identify the wisdom traditions that various settlers brought with them from the countries they left. And, are there wisdom traditions of different groups particular to local ecosystems that continue to be carried forward.?

5   STEM teachers need to meet in larger groups to discuss how to revitalize or create new wisdom traditions in collaboration with various local groups centered on various ecologically sustainable cultural practices such as the local Slow Food group, the efforts to form intentional communities living off the grid, and the networks within the local community that are carrying forward the various traditions within the arts, craft skills, and knowledge.

9

HELPING TO PROTECT STUDENTS FROM THE EXCESSES OF SCIENTISM IN TODAY'S WORLD

Scientism needs to be understood as the failure of scientists to recognize that their mode of inquiry is too limited for understanding the symbolic worlds of culture, and that this limitation is overlooked as they adopt the taken for granted assumptions about a linear form of progress, a culture-free view of the rational process, that technologies are both culturally neutral and the basis of progress, and that data and facts have an objective status free of historical and culturally specific linguistic influences—and that many are driven by a deeply held messianic drive to save the world from ignorance. This drive is rooted in a will to power that Friedrich Nietzsche explained as "our need to interpret the world; our drive and their For and Against. Every drive is a kind of lust to rule; each one has its perspective that it would like to compel all other drives to accept as the norm" (Kaufmann, 1968, 267).

The influence of scientism has extended into every effort to move the Industrial Revolution to new levels of efficiency and profits, as well as into medicine, education, agriculture, built environments, foreign policy and military technologies, and now the digital revolution that is changing life in fundamental ways that extend well beyond the efficiencies, conveniences, and new forms of empowerment that are so widely celebrated. The two areas where scientism has had its greatest impact in putting at risk the possibility of an ecologically sustainable future are the Industrial Revolution and the Digital Revolution. A strong case can be made that the digital revolution is a continuation of the Industrial Revolution that began in the Midlands of England over two centuries ago. When assessing the differences in how these two revolutions are threatening life as we know it, it is important to treat them separately—while keeping in mind that both are based on the same deep cultural assumptions that this is a human-centered world, that the individual is the basic social unit, and that market forces dictate the direction of progressive and now evolutionary change.

Focusing on how scientism in brain research ignores the cultural/linguistic ecologies that sustain all life-forming processes, including that of the individual, by reducing the exercise of intelligence to mechanistic process occurring in the brain, leads to a different set of reform priorities. These as well as other perspectives on the cultural impacts of scientism are less important in terms of what STEM teachers might be able to achieve if they stay focused on the dangers resulting from the globalization of the West's industrial/consumer dependent culture, and on how the digital revolution contributes to both serious security issues as well as the intergenerational knowledge that will become more critical as natural systems begin to fail.

The globalization of the industrial revolution, and the consumer dependent form of individualism it requires, are chiefly responsible for the rate and scope of changes occurring in the Earth's natural ecologies that are leading to civil wars, forcing hundreds of millions of people further into poverty, and that are killing off species and destroying habitats. The current migration of people northward into central Europe, as well as from other parts of the world, is only a fraction of what will happen as sources of water and protein become even more limited. Global warming is the second catastrophe that is changing our future prospects. For example, the melting of the glaciers in the South American Andes that are the primary source of water for millions of people, which are estimated to be completely gone over the next 30 to 40 years, is just one example of how the shortage of water will become more critical in the immediate decades ahead—in India, Pakistan, the Middle East, China, and most other regions of the world. The ecological crisis has many faces, depending upon the region of the world as well as the population density and lifestyle of the people.

The changes resulting from the digital revolution are mostly understood by the wider public, by businesses and educators, and by governments as yet further examples of progress. But like everything connected with the speed of change within the industry, this perception is beginning to change—especially as the number of cyber attacks on governments and the hacking of technological secrets of corporations increases. In their book, *The Future of Violence: Robots and Germs, Hackers and Drones* (2015) Benjamin Wittes and Gabriella Blum observe what should have been obvious to the computer scientists doing the pioneering work of changing the foundations of culture from the sensory world of patterns that connect memories, diverse semiotic systems of representation, to the abstract number combinations of 0s and 1s. How is it possible to hack what is communicated orally, as well as the interpretative frameworks that are taken for granted within a culture as well as between cultures, the patterns of moral reciprocity, and the narratives encoded in dance and music? By reducing cultural traditions to context-free computer codes it then became possible for anyone anywhere in the world, as Witte and Blum note, to use powerful computer systems to reproduce the digital patterns and thus to gain access to what previously was considered protected by the same binary language.

The state can no longer provide protection from the raiders in this new mono-linguistic abstract world. Differences in cultural languages have long been understood as often impenetrable by outsiders, which was the case when the speakers of Navajo were used during World War II to prevent the Japanese from intercepting messages. The meaning of the spoken word changes depending upon local contexts, nuances even in the tone of voice and patterns of meta-communication, status relationships, and uses of silences. All of this is lost as the ecology of emergent differences, relationships and co-dependencies are replaced by binary codes that can be used to steal identities, access bank accounts, spread misinformation that affects one's life chances, create data records of past performances and all electronically mediated behaviors that can be sold to corporations and governmental agencies which will come under even more fine grained surveillance as the Internet of Everything collects data on behaviors in your home—including the bedroom. The prospects of living in a techno-fascist future, where even the energy grids, financial systems, and personal technologies as well as those used in the workplace can be taken over by hackers as well as the country's security agencies has not really penetrated the consciousness of today's youth who are still mesmerized by computer games, the ability to send hundreds of text messages to faceless entities, and to be in constant contact with a network of others who find their sense of meaning and worth in the number of messages they receive.

But as students leave the security of classrooms and campuses and enter the world of work they will begin to encounter another achievement of computer scientists who are working in collaboration with the corporate world to attain its goal of greater efficiencies and profits. That is, they will begin to wake up to how the sub-culture of computer scientists is developing the technologies that not only replace humans in the workplace but are also developing super-intelligent computers that will take over more of human decision making. Careers in law, medicine, journalism, law enforcement, accounting, education (including professors), military, counseling, are being taken over by algorithms and robotic systems, with computer scientists such Ray Kurzweil claiming that within a few decades most work will be done by computer systems.

Students moving into the adult world will also be encountering the ecological changes resulting from the billions of tons of carbon dioxide and other greenhouse gases released into the atmosphere that are changing the chemistry of the world's oceans, depleting the world's fisheries as coral systems die off, and as global warming and the mining of aquifers limits the availability of water. The current generation of students who will still be alive in the latter decades of this century are still entrapped by the progress-oriented and individually centered mindset that provided conceptual direction to the industrial revolution. Their public school teachers and university professors, while increasingly focused on technological solutions to the ecological crisis, continue to ignore questioning the cultural assumptions they inherited from their mentors. Indoctrinated to accept the abstractions learned in universities about free markets, being an autonomous individual, and the authority of print-based cultural storage and data, they will enter a world where jobs are widely available writing code that will further displace humans in the work place. The cycle will then repeat itself of advancing the ability of digital technologies to replace human skills and judgments, while increasing the number of people who do not have access to meaningful work and thus the ability to support themselves. All forms of resistance will, in the name of national security, be under electronic surveillance.

To recall a key characteristic of scientism: it involves using knowledge acquired through the scientific method to introduce changes in the culture—changes that are not subject to the safeguards used in scientific experiments, and to peer review. Nor are the cultural changes subject to the democratic process. The changes, such as developing algorithms that displace humans in the workplace, and developing electronic surveillance technologies such as Stingray that mimic cell phone towers that force cell phones in the vicinity to connect to the device. The changes are simply understood as yet another example of progress, with little attention being given to cultural traditions that are being lost beyond any point of recovery.

The industrial revolution, which is an example of scientism on a massive scale, has also changed the chemistry of living organisms and now the Earth's ecosystems. The question for STEM teachers is how can they help students, who will still be living into the last decades of this century, to protect themselves in the event that the worst case scenarios become a reality? The answer to this question requires stepping outside of their role as a teacher of science, technology, engineering, and mathematics—though before stepping outside these roles it is hoped that they enable students to learn about the limits of science, the cultural transforming nature of technology, the need to introduce ecological design principles into engineering, and the appropriate and inappropriate uses of mathematics.

Why STEM Teachers Need to Take on the Role of Mentors

Unlike teachers responsible for other areas of the curriculum, such as English and literature, history, social studies, economics, and so forth, STEM teachers are the only ones knowledgeable about the rate and scale of changes occurring in natural systems. Indeed, the non-STEM teachers will be reinforcing the silences and misconceptions they learned from their professors across the academic disciplines. And in reproducing the silences and misconceptions of their professors, they will not be introducing students to the language issues, the taken for granted ways in which most of culture is learned, and the ways in which scientism leads to forms of progress that undermine local decision making and knowledge of the traditions that need to be intergenerationally renewed. Nor will teachers in these non-science areas be able to help students understand the cultural myths that surround the development of technologies. Hopefully, the reforms being suggested here for a culturally and linguistically informed approach to educating STEM teachers will place them in critical leadership positions within schools.

What is being recommended here is that STEM teachers should adopt the role of mentors in sustainable living. This means introducing students to what has been widely ignored because of the mind-altering noise of the consumer and technology dependent culture. Namely, the cultural and natural commons that have been carried forward since the first humans wandered the savannas of what is now called Africa. As I have explained elsewhere (2000, 2003, 2006, 2011, 2011, 2012, 2013, 2014, 2015) in a common sense and ethnographically informed vocabulary that made little sense to colleagues conditioned to thinking about various forms of emancipation and the power of critical inquiry, everyone participates in the cultural commons of their family and primary social group, as well as within the cultural commons of their ethnic group and larger society. The largely non-monetized skills, knowledge, and patterns of mutual support that range across a wide spectrum of cultural activities, and that reframe the meaning of wealth to mean the skills and creative activities that add to the quality of life within the cultural commons, are what STEM teachers, in their role as mentors in sustainable living, need to bring to the attention of their students. This simply requires relying upon the ethnographies introduced in earlier discussions of becoming aware of cultural patterns that are otherwise taken for granted and thus reproduce the misconceptions of a past that was not ecologically informed.

Helping students make explicit and give close attention to cultural patterns will lead to recognizing the mutual support systems that intergenerationally renew the cultural commons exist in different forms, from groups focused on food security issues to the networks of creative artists, to groups collectively working to conserve habitats and species. As they focus more on developing their talents and the sharing of skills, rather than purchasing entertainment, processed foods, and the skills of the elites that promote the culture of dependence and consumerism, they rely less on the money economy. They also have a smaller ecological footprint as they rely more on materials grown and developed locally. As communities of shared interests they support mutual exchanges and bartering—even local currencies.

The intergenerational renewal of the cultural commons exists in urban, suburban, and rural areas. They are largely passed forward through face-to-face communication and involve different networks of shared interests. It may be a musical group, a farmers' market, weavers and potters in the community, social justice activists, people who carry forward different traditions of healing, mentors in a variety of the creative arts, and skilled craftspersons who work with metal, stone, and wood. Renewing the cultural commons may take on limited forms such as keeping family holidays with traditional foods and keeping alive an art form, or it can be a larger community where most people such as in the intentional communities in different parts of the world share a commitment to living less consumer-dependent and environmentally destructive lives. In these communities, wealth is understood as possessing talents and skills that enrich the lives of others.

What is especially important about cultural commons activities, and intentional communities where the individually centered values and competition of the industrial cultures are being replaced by the values of mutual support, is that they are welcoming communities for those who are being discarded by the industrial culture that is in the early stage of making the transition from human workers to digital programmed work forces. One of the ironies of educational and social reformers who are focused on overcoming poverty is that they have largely ignored how the curriculum of the public schools could be used to introduce students to the diversity of cultural commons activities within their communities, to understand the cultural commons of various ethnic groups, and to recognize how the cultural commons are being undermined by different technologies and market liberal values.

STEM teachers, in effect, should possess a clearer understanding of the benefits of the sciences but at the same time be more aware of how scientific knowledge is being taken over by market forces such as we are now witnessing as computer scientists align themselves with corporate agendas for amassing wealth and political power. Their role as mentors in how to live more ecologically sustainable lives, as well as how to survive in a world that will become more chaotic in the decades ahead as natural systems break down in the face of massive human demands, is to encourage students to learn about how advanced technologies are impacting people's lives in communities as well as how revitalizing different cultural commons traditions is leading to better physical health and states of mind. This is not something that can be learned from books and from computer programs, but instead from students talking with mentors in the community, with older people who remember how healthy foods were raised and how to live less chemically dependent lives.

As pointed out earlier, it is nearly impossible for STEM teachers to introduce students to the nature of natural systems, including how they are being degraded at a rate that will impact the students' future prospects, without raising real concerns that could lead to anger, depression, and a desire to strike back at the selfishness and ignorance of adults. Encouraging students to learn about the importance of the cultural commons in alleviating poverty, loneliness, and a sense of existential purposelessness is a responsibility of STEM teachers taking on the role of mentor in how to best prepare for the uncertainties of the future—and in giving students a basis for hope.

As the scientism of those within the sub-culture of computer science leads to integrating all aspects of daily life into the network of microprocessors central to the Internet of Everything, there will be few ways for youth entering adulthood to escape becoming part of a data file stored somewhere in a cloud. Their performance, as well as what they studied in school, will have already become part of their data file. All electronic devices, used in decisions about managing their household to physical movements as well as Internet communication with others, will provide anonymous Others with information on how to manipulate consumer choices, send warnings to police agencies engaged in "predicting policing," and information to potential employers who will make decisions based on their taken for granted ideological frameworks still shaped by the cultural assumptions of past eras when the environment was understood as endlessly exploitable.

STEM teachers need to engage students in discussions of the cultural practices that cannot be electronically monitored. The awareness that electronic technologies such as satellites and GPS systems can be hacked has led the U.S. Navy to reinstate learning navigational skills by using sextants and nautical almanacs, which had been dropped in the 1990s as no longer needed. As STEM teachers engage students in considering the cultural patterns that cannot be hacked it will become increasingly clear that participating in the local cultural commons is a safe haven from hackers and surveillance technologies generally. Face-to-face communication, like the use of the sextant, cannot be hacked or the focus of the hidden surveillance systems. So then the question becomes, what are the activities within the cultural commons that are dependent upon face-to-face communication: These activities include face-to-face conversations that lead to learning skills and knowledge of how to grow and prepare food, healing practices, knowledge, skills, and protocols governing various creative traditions, mentoring in developing craft skills, narratives of past achievements and moral missteps, passing on the rules of games, the vocabularies necessary for recognizing injustices and forms of exploitation. Other activities within the cultural commons include the use of barter and patterns of mutual exchange—and even the use of local currencies. Even the political exchanges that occur in local decision making are free of surveillance as long as they are not electronically recorded. In effect, the cultural commons activities, which may occupy only part of a person's daily life or encompass a more cultural commons-centered daily life, represent the safety zones from the policing characteristics that the sub-culture of computer scientists have left as their legacy of scientism.

STEM teachers also need to engage students in learning about how ethnic cultures that have stored their knowledge in oral traditions, rather than in print and now computer-based systems, have been able to conserve the basis of their identities, patterns of mutual support, skills and knowledge, and ecological wisdom. What is especially important to consider is how many ethnic cultures are being indoctrinated to adopt the West's emphasis on consumerism, dependence upon the digital technologies, and the values that support the myth of progress. Indeed, one of the challenges STEM teachers face is in recognizing when they are promoting the cultural changes that expand the influence of scientism.

Questions for Students to Consider

1   As the digital revolution is introducing many changes that further marginalize the security of the average person, in the work place, in making decisions about what cultural traditions need to be intergenerationally renewed, and in avoiding being hacked and brought under constant surveillance by corporations and governments, ask students to identify the range of activities within the cultural commons that do not involve an electronic footprint.

2   Discuss with students examples of cultural commons activities that exist in urban centers. These may range from sports clubs, artistic groups, places where narratives are shared, where people use vacant lots to grow and share food, where students are mentored in how to provide support for others in need. Also, discuss the ways in which climate change, as well as digital technologies, are affecting these largely non-monetized activities and relationships.

3   Using as an example the vocabularies that support the root metaphor of mechanism as an explanatory framework even for understanding organic phenomenon, ask the students to identify the vocabularies that support the root metaphors of individualism and progress. After they identify the web of supporting vocabulary for each of the root metaphors, have them discuss why so little attention is given to the traditions that are reenacted and modified in their everyday cultural experience. Also, have them discuss traditions that are now being overturned by digital technologies—and why these traditions cannot be recovered. To ensure that students do not mistake this discussion as an attempt to get them to embrace all traditions, and thus to resist reforms, make the point that the intergenerational knowledge and skills that enable people live less consumer dependent lives are examples of traditions.

4   Discuss what there is about the scientific mode of inquiry that leads so few scientists to consider important cultural traditions that are being overturned. Is this a general problem within the science community, or is it a problem for specific areas of science? What separates environmental scientists from computer scientists in terms of being aware of what needs to be conserved?

10

RETHINKING SOCIAL JUSTICE ISSUES WITHIN AN ECO-JUSTICE CONCEPTUAL AND MORAL FRAMEWORK

The merging of a series of scientific discoveries and new technologies with capitalism enabled the Industrial Revolution to displace the guild systems of the Middle Ages, and the craft-based economies that fit the rhymes of community life. The resulting impact of scientism has been a continued source of social injustices. Exploiting child labor, paying as low wages as possible, subjecting workers to dangerous conditions, and fiercely resisting worker strikes are synonymous with the Industrial Revolution up until the early part of the 20th century. Better education and media coverage, as well as a Congress more willing to respond to public pressure led to many gains, as well as reversals such as introducing the scientific management of the production process. Beyond the social injustices in the workplace, there has always been discrimination—against women, the already poor seeking to escape limited opportunities in other parts of the world such as the slaves from Africa, Irish, Italians, Jews, Chinese, Poles, Germans, and, more recently, Hispanics and Latinos from south of the border. Having a foreign name, darker skin color, being less fluent in English, engaging in non-WASP traditions meant being part of the class subjected to discrimination and economic exploitation. Fortunately, social justice gains have been made by many of these groups—though much still needs to be done especially among the indigenous Americans, Hispanic/Latino, African American, and groups still immigrating to this country. Part of the continued discrimination can be attributed to racial and ethnic prejudices rooted in the language into which succeeding generations have been socialized as well as in the inability of many marginalized groups to escape from generations of poverty.

Against this background history of discrimination and prejudice scientism is again adding to the obstacles facing social justice reformers. The influence of educators in contributing to a more socially just society has been largely limited to changing stereotypical thinking that limited people's opportunity to express their talents, and to influencing the thinking of employers. But they have had little influence on the even more critical aspects of the industrial/consumer dependent culture that has been changing the chemistry of the world's ecosystems. The billions of tons of carbon dioxide, as well as other chemicals put into the atmosphere and on the land, are also the unintended consequences of scientism. While contributing to the exploitation of the environment in the name of progress, scientism has been a powerful force in manipulating people's wants, in creating endless products loaded with life threatening chemicals. For-hire scientists have played an important role in advancing the profit oriented agenda of the processed food and pharmaceutical industries (which appear to collude in damaging people's health and then selling them the needed drugs), and in using engineering and mathematics to calculate the rate of profits from huge mineral extraction operations and other environmental abuses.

The question educational reformers who still think of social injustice in terms of access to work, to education, and to political participation have not been considering is the double bind of enabling marginalized groups to join on more equitable terms the middle class consumer society. That is, the social justice educational reformers ignored the ecologically unsustainable nature of the economic system that continues to poison the environment that all life depends upon. And they have also ignored how gaining access to the middle class too often involves the loss of the cultural commons of the students' family and ethnic group. Ironically, the connections between upward mobility that required integration into the mainstream values and ways of thinking, and the loss of ethnic traditions have been represented as one of the success stories of America.

Yet the question that becomes more urgent is whether those who have recently joined the consumer-dependent middle class, as well as today's powerless and economically disadvantaged social groups, will survive as the ecological crisis deepens. One of the unintended consequences of the innovations of scientists, technologists, and capitalists who are now promoting their ecologically destructive market system on a global scale is that the economically marginalized and politically powerless who should be the focus of social justice reforms will be impacted the greatest. They are more exposed to having their lives further impoverished by climate change that is leading to extreme weather conditions in terms of floods, drought, and forest fires. As the homes and limited possessions of the already poor are destroyed by floods and their work limited by droughts, they will have few resources to recover. And they have less influence on the federal and state agencies that provide different forms of relief.

The cultural changes resulting from the Digital Revolution, which again was motivated by how Enlightenment thinkers' assumed that basing everyday life on the mode of thinking acclaimed by other elites, that is critical rationality of the individual as well as science and technology, would lead to progress. This unexamined assumption was encoded in the metaphorical language that guided the thinking of the early computer scientists, mathematicians, engineers, and now the developers of computer software. Lacking the necessary culturally informed theory frameworks, as well as vocabularies for making explicit the historical taken for granted cultural assumptions within their sub-culture, which are also necessary for understanding what they are undermining in the larger culture, the ideologically driven elite of computer scientists, technologists, engineers, and capitalists are changing the foundations of what previously represented core values of American society.

What is now the hallmark of the digital revolution, which represents gains in efficiencies in medical technologies, as well as in the fields of journalism, law, business and manufacturing, communication, scientific research, and so forth, is the effort to create algorithms for replacing human decision making and skills in as many areas of life as possible. The current challenge facing those working in the highly funded computer research and development centers is to develop computer systems such as robots and especially algorithms that can automatically make decisions based on the vast quantities of data that the surveillance technologies now record and store in the cloud. Robots are replacing skilled workers, and even taking over from unskilled and underpaid workers. One has only to look at the role of workers in a major industry such as Amazon. But it's the algorithms, the decision making software that utilize data from work related contexts that have been digitally coded, and now have the ability to constantly adjust their own decision making by taking into account changes occurring in different designated environments. Scientism (the mix of ideology and technological innovations) is now displacing white-collar workers. Algorithms now make decisions in accounting, hiring new personnel, banking decisions about who should receive loans, diagnosing an illness, guiding self-driving cars and military drones, and even writing story lines for the media. As computer scientists are now working on how differences in the English language should influence the algorithm's decision making process they will be even more widely used in society—and thus further the spread of scientism that leads to even fewer jobs.

The expansion of work opportunities for the small number of highly yet narrowly educated graduates of today's universities may represent an opportunity for a few from the marginalized groups to advance, and to participate in the development of digital technologies that are changing not only consciousness (where long-term memories are disappearing) but also bringing more of daily life under constant surveillance that puts society on the slippery slope leading to a police state where police and other governmental agencies are already practicing "predictive policing."

The current form of scientism, that is the cultural changes introduced by the Digital Revolution, is already closing the door on making further social justice gains, especially now that the global ecological crisis is leading to massive numbers of people being driven from their homes and environments too devastated to support them (now estimated at over 60 million worldwide). There are fewer jobs, with even fewer jobs in the future as software programs that will further reduce the need for employees represent one of the fastest growing and profitable markets. Unlike the 70s and 80s when social justice reformers were dealing mostly with prejudices and systemic forms of discrimination, now the world of opportunities is being significantly reduced by how computer scientists and their colleagues equate progress with the globalization of technologies that elevate data above all other forms of knowledge. What is noteworthy about these cultural change agents is that they ignore what needs to be conserved such as civil liberties and the largely non-monetized intergenerational knowledge and skills that will become increasing important in the immediate decades ahead.

There are other changes that now face social justice activists. Those who gain the most from the surveillance culture that was never voted on by the people are the corporations, police, and other governmental security agencies. In the past there were a variety of ways to protest various forms of social injustice. Street demonstrations, picket lines and worker strikes, speeches by people such as Cesar Chavez of the United Farm Workers, leading feminist spokespersons, activists promoting "Black Lives Matter" and other social justice issues, indigenous leaders, and so forth were under constant surveillance by police and the FBI. But the police-state mentality has now moved to a higher level of efficiency in tracking people's political activism. Even classroom teachers who speak out about social injustices are now being monitored. And faculty who discuss with students the social injustices experienced by Palestinians are now being monitored and subjected to pressure by the threat that donations will be withheld from their university. The ability of governmental agencies to use software programs that provide access in real time to ongoing cell phone conversations represents the near ultimate loss of privacy—with the total loss of privacy occurring as the sensors that are part of the Internet of Everything become more widely incorporated into homes.

That so few people recognize that the personal conveniences that accompany the digital revolution are being attained by giving up their personal privacy and security from hackers is a measure of the failure of the current educational system that leaves people totally indifferent to how scientism is changing their lives. As fish stocks decline further from overfishing and from the acidification of the world's oceans, as global warming disrupts agriculture, and as the growing unrest across the world's population resulting from the combination of increasing unemployment and the loss of basic resources, concern about social injustice is likely to be eclipsed by the social chaos resulting from the sheer numbers of homeless and desperate people. The hundreds of thousands of desperate people fleeing from the Middle East represent social injustice issues that are on a scale that even governments are unable to address.

As mentioned before, STEM teachers educated to understand the cultural issues, as well as how past expressions of scientism are now contributing to the further limiting life sustaining possibilities, now need to take on another task. And this one is directly related to integrating a knowledge of the students' inherited traditions of the cultural commons into the curriculum—including helping students become explicitly aware of the range of intergenerational non-monetized activities and relationships within their family, ethnic group, and within the larger culture. This understanding of what has been missing in the curricula of public schools and universities now needs to be shared with the many social groups and agencies that are attempting to ensure food security and housing for the poor and politically powerless. Hopefully, other teachers will become aware of how the Common Core Curriculum further undermines the intergenerational knowledge and skills that are still carried forward within families and ethnic groups. Even the poor and destitute continue to depend upon the knowledge and survival skills that are intergenerationally passed forward.

The doors to achieving social justice will be increasingly closed by the panic that will accompany the deepening of the ecological crisis, as well as by the computer scientists and the other technological elites who are striving to replace human decision making, moral responsibility, and the world's many wisdom traditions with digital machines. Their ultimate goal is to create forms of artificial intelligence that operate independently from human intelligence and thus from the democratic process.

Readers find what I have sketched here is an excessively alarmist view of what will occur over the next 50 years when many of the students in the early grades, as well as the youth without homes that are struggling to find their next meal, are still alive. In clarifying for yourself what lies ahead, consider the rate at which the world's oceans are becoming more acidic (and are predicted to reach a pH level of 7.8 by the end of the century) and the resulting destruction of the oceans' food webs, the rate at which glaciers are melting and aquifers are being depleted that will leave hundreds of millions of people without adequate sources of water, the rate at which habitats and species are disappearing, and the scale and rate of forest fires that are releasing even more carbon dioxide that adds to the rate of global warming. The 50 years into the future scenario that today's youth will find as the legacy we and earlier progress oriented generations have left them must also take into account the further displacement of humans and their wisdom traditions by technocrats whose life work is centered on creating computer systems that will take over their own design thus achieving Ray Kurzweil's vision of machines displacing humans in the process of evolution.

If you have thoughts of challenging the techno-fascist slippery slope we are headed down by this more totalitarian form of scientism, you would be advised not to use any electronic technology to communicate your concerns, as the data collectors are not only listening, but will also know the physical location of you and the others you are communicating with. The loss of privacy means there will be no place to hide. To recall the earlier discussions of the root causes and nature of scientism, it results from the failure of scientists, technologists, and engineers to understand the cultures into which their innovations are introduced, and to recognize what the Enlightenment thinkers overlooked. Even our most progress-oriented elites are still in the grip of the past.

BIBLIOGRAPHY

Apffel-Marglin, F. 1998. *The Spirit of Regeneration: Andean Culture Confronting Western Notions of Development.* London: Zed Publishers.

Bateson, G. 1972. *Steps to An Ecology of Mind.* New York: Ballantine.

Berger, P. and T. Luckmann. 1966. *The Social Construction of Reality.* New York: Anchor Press.

Berry, W. 2000. *Life is a Miracle: An Essay Against a Modern Superstition.* Washington, D.C.: Counterpoint Press.

Bible: Book of Genesis

Bowers, C. 1997. *The Culture of Denial: Why the Environmental Movement Needs a Strategy for Reforming Universities and Public Schools.* Albany: State University of New York Press.

——. 2000. *Let Them Eat Data: How Computers Affect Education, Cultural Diversity, and the Prospects of Ecological Sustainability.* Athens: University of Georgia Press.

——. 2003. *Mindful Conservatism: Rethinking the Ideological and Educational Basis of an Ecologically Sustainable Future.* Lanham, Maryland: Rowman & Littlefield.

——. 2006. *Revitalizing the Common: Cultural and Educational Sites of Resistance and Affirmation.* Lanham, Maryland: Lexington Books.

——. 2011. *Perspectives on the Ideas of Gregory Bateson, Ecological Intelligence, and Educational Reforms.* Eugene, OR: Eco-Justice Press.

——. 2011. *University Reform in an Era of Global Warming.* Eugene, OR: Eco-Justice Press.

——. 2012. *The Way Forward: Educational Reforms that Focus on the Cultural Commons and the Linguistic Roots of the Ecological/Cultural Crises.* Eugene, OR: Eco-Justice Press.

——. 2013 *In the Grip of the Past: Educational Reforms that Address What Should be Changed and What Should be Conserved.* Eugene, OR: Eco Justice Press.

——. 2014 *The False Promises of the Digital Revolution: How Computers are Changing Education, Work, and International Development in Ways that are Ecologically Unsustainable.* New York: Peter Lang.

——. 2015. *An Ecological and Cultural Critique of the Common Core Curriculum.* New York: Peter Lang.

Carson, R. 1962. *Silent Spring.* New York: Houghton Mifflin.

Crick, F. 1994. *The Astonishing Hypothesis: The Scientific Search for the Soul*. New York: Scribners.

Dawkins, R. 1976. *The Selfish Gene*. Oxford: Oxford University Press.

Diamandis, P. and S. Kotler. 2012. *Abundance: The Future is Better than You Think*. New York: Free Press.

Dissanayake, E. 1990. *What is Art For?* Seattle: University of Washington Press.

——. 1995. *Homo Aestheticus*. Seattle: University of Washington Press.

Drexler, K. 2013. *Radical Abundance: How a Revolution in Nanotechnology Will Change Civilization*. Nook e-book.

Dyson, G. 1998. *Darwin Among the Machines: The Evolution of Global Intelligence*. New York: Basic Books.

Ellul, J. 1964. *The Technological Society*. New York: Vintage.

Geertz, C. 1977. *The Interpretation of Cultures*. New York: Basic Books.

Gelernter, D. 2014, "The Closing of the Scientific Mind." *Commentary*. January 3, pp. 17–25.

Goody, J. 1977. Th*e Domestication of the Savage Mind*. Cambridge: Cambridge University Press.

Hardin, G. 1968. "The Tragedy of the Commons". *Science*. 162: 1243–1248.

Havelock, E. 1986. *The Muse Learns to Write: Reflections on Orality and Literacy from Antiquity to the Present*. New Haven: Yale University Press.

Hawking, S. 1996. *A Brief History of Time*. London: Bantam Dell Pu.

Heidegger, M. 1977. *The Question Concerning Technology and Other Essays*. New York: Norton.

Ihde, D. 1979. *Technics and Praxis*. Dordrecht, Holland: D. Reidel Publishing.

Kaku, M. 2011. *Physics of the Future: How Science Will Shape Human Destiny and Our Daily Lives by the Year 2100*. New York: Doubleday.

——. 2014. *The Future of the Mind: The Scientific Quest to Understand, Enhance, and Empower the Mind*. New York: Anchor Books.

Kane, S. 1994. *Wisdom of the Mythtellers*. Peterborough, Canada: Broadview Press.

Kaufmann, W, (editor) 1968, *The Will to Power*. New York: Vintage.

Kolbert, E. 2014, *The Sixth Extinction: An Unnatural History*. New York: Henry Holt.

Kurzweil, R. 1999. *The Age of Spiritual Machines: When Computers Exceed Human Intelligence*. New York: Viking.

——. 2005. *The Singularity Is Near: When Humans Transcend Biology*. New York: Viking.

——. 2012. *How to Create a Mind: The Secret of Human Thought Revealed*. New York: Viking.

Lakoff, G, and M. Johnson, M. 1980. *Metaphors We Live By*. Chicago: University of Chicago Press.

——. 1999. *Philosophy in the Flesh: The Embodied Mind and Its Challenge to Western Thought*. New York: Basic Books.

Lawlor, R. 1991. *Voices of the First Day: Awakening in the Aboriginal Dreamtime*. Rochester, VT: Inner Traditions International.

Leopold, A. 1949. *A Sand County Almanac and Sketches Here and There*. New York: Oxford University Press.

Maunakea, S. 2015, (personal communication).

Moravec, H. 1990. *Mind Children: The Future of Robot and Human Intelligence*. Cambridge, MA: Harvard University Press.

——. 2000. *Robot: Mere Machine to Transcendent Mind*: New York: Oxford University Press.

Mosco, V. 2014. *To the Cloud: Big Data in a Turbulent World.* Boulder, CO: Paradigm Publishers.

Muehlhauser, L. 2013. *Facing the Intellectual Explosion.* Kindle e-book.

Mumford, L. 1934. *Technics and Civilization.* New York: Harcourt, Brace.

——. 1967. *Technics and Human Development.* New York: Harcourt, Brace.

——. 1970. *The Pentagon of Power: The Myth of the Machine.* New York: Harcourt, Brace Javanovich.

Nhat Hanh. T. 2002. *No Death, No Fear.* New York: Riverhead Books.

Nichols, W. 2014. *Blue Mind: The Surprising Science that Shows How Being Near, In, or Under Water can Make You Happier, Healthier, More Connected, and Better at What You do.* New York: Little, Brown.

Ong, W. 1982. *Orality and Literacy: the Technologizing of the Word.* New York: Methuen Publishers.—2002 cited in text.

Orwell, G. 1949. *Nineteen Eighty-Four.* New York: Harcourt Brace.

Putnam, R. 2014. *Our Kids: The American Dream in Crisis.* New York: Simon & Schuster.

Rand, A. 1961. *The Virtue of Selfishness.* New York: Signet.

Reddy, M. 1979. "The Conduit Metaphor—A Case of Frame Conflict in Our Language About Language". In Andrew Ortony (Ed.) *Metaphor and Thought.* (pp. 284–323) Cambridge: Cambridge University Press.

Rengifo, Vasquez, G. 1998. "The AYLLU." In *The Spirit of Regeneration: Andean Culture Confronting Western Notions of Development.* London: Zed Books.

Sagan, C. 1997. *The Demon-Haunted World: Science as a Candle in the Dark.* London: Headline Book Publishing.

Schmidt, E. and J. Cohen. 2013. *The New Digital Age: Reshaping the Future of People, Nations, and Business.* New York: Alfred A. Knopf.

Shils, E. 1981. *Tradition.* Chicago: University of Chicago Press.

Shiva, V. 2005. *Earth Democracy: Justice, Sustainability and Peace.* Cambridge, Mass.: South End Press.

Silver, L. 2007. *Remaking Eden: How Genetic Engineering and Cloning will Transform the American Family.* New York: Harper Perennial.

Smith, H. 1991. *The World's Religions.* New York: Harper One.

Soulé, M. 1995. "The Social Siege of Nature," in *Reinventing Nature? Responses to Postmodern Deconstruction*, by M. Soulé and Gary Lease (editors). Washington D.C.: Island Press. pp. 137–170.

Spretnak, C. 2011. *Relational Reality: New Discoveries of Interrelatedness that are Transforming the World.* Topsham, ME: Green Horizon Books.

Stock, G. 1993. *Metaman: The Merging of Humans and Machines into a Global Superorganism.* New York: Doubleday.

Wilson, E. 1998. *Consilience: The Unity of Knowledge.* New York: Alfred A. Knopf.

Wittes, B. and G. Blum. 2015. *The Future of Violence: Robots and Germs, Hackers and Drones.* New York: Basic Books.

Woolfolk, A. 1993. *Educational Psychology.* Boston: Allyn & Bacon.

Worster, D. 1977. *Nature's Economy: A History of Ecological Ideas.* Cambridge: Cambridge University Press.

INDEX